Portrait of

Cuba

Turner Publishing, Inc.

A Subsidiary of Turner Broadcasting Systems, Inc.

One CNN Center, Box 105366

Atlanta, Georgia 30348-5366

Michael J. Walsh
Design, Photography & Production Director

James W. Porges
Senior Editor

Marian G. Llord
Copy Editor

Larry Larson
Coordinating Editor

Karen E. Robinson
Design & Production Assistant

Lisa Saylan
Photo Research

Library of Congress Catalog Number
91-066125

First Edition
10 9 8 7 6 5 4 3 2 1
ISBN 1-878685-07-4 (hardcover)

Distributed by Andrews & McMeel
4900 Main Street
Kansas City, Missouri 64112

Designed and produced on a Macintosh IIci computer using
QuarkExpress 3.0 and Aldus FreeHand 3.0.
Typeface used: Adobe Cochin family.
Color separations by Color Response Inc., Charlotte, North Carolina.
Printed on 100# Mounte Matte Potlatch paper with a Komori sheet-fed, four-color press.
Printing by Arcata Graphics Book Group, Kingsport, Tennessee.

Table of Contents

FOREWORD

Map of Cuba 4

Foreword 6

Photographic Foreword 8

SECTION 1 : EARLY HISTORY

I. The Ever Faithful Isle 38

SECTION 2 : ENTER FIDEL

II. They Came From the Hills 70

III. Castro The Man 94

IV. The Paradox of Revolution 110

V. Embracing the Bear 118

VI. In the Shadow of the Giant 126

VII. Cuba & the Third World 140

VIII. Race, Religion & the Revolution 146

SECTION 3 : CUBA TODAY

IX. An Economy of Circumstance 168

X. Cuba in a Changing World 174

XI. An Uncertain Future 188

Illustration by Ken Mowry

~ Foreword

THIS IS A PIVOTAL TIME IN CUBAN HISTORY, AS SIGNIFICANT AS ITS discovery by Columbus in 1492, its liberation from Spanish rule at the turn of the century and the Revolution of 1959. Only ninety miles off the coast of Florida, Cuba remains an island shrouded in mystery and misconception due to more than three decades of Cold War circumstance. Americans know little about this island or the Cubans themselves, a proud people with a colorful and passionate heritage. As the post-Cold War world continues to evolve, Cuba must modify its economic and political system if it is to meet the challenges of a vastly changed world. It seems an appropriate occasion to take a closer look at this island whose history is so closely linked to our own. Our hope is that the reader will come away with a lasting impression of Cuba and an appreciation of its vibrant, enduring culture.

Text by

Wayne S.

Smith

~

Photographs

by Michael

Reagan

~

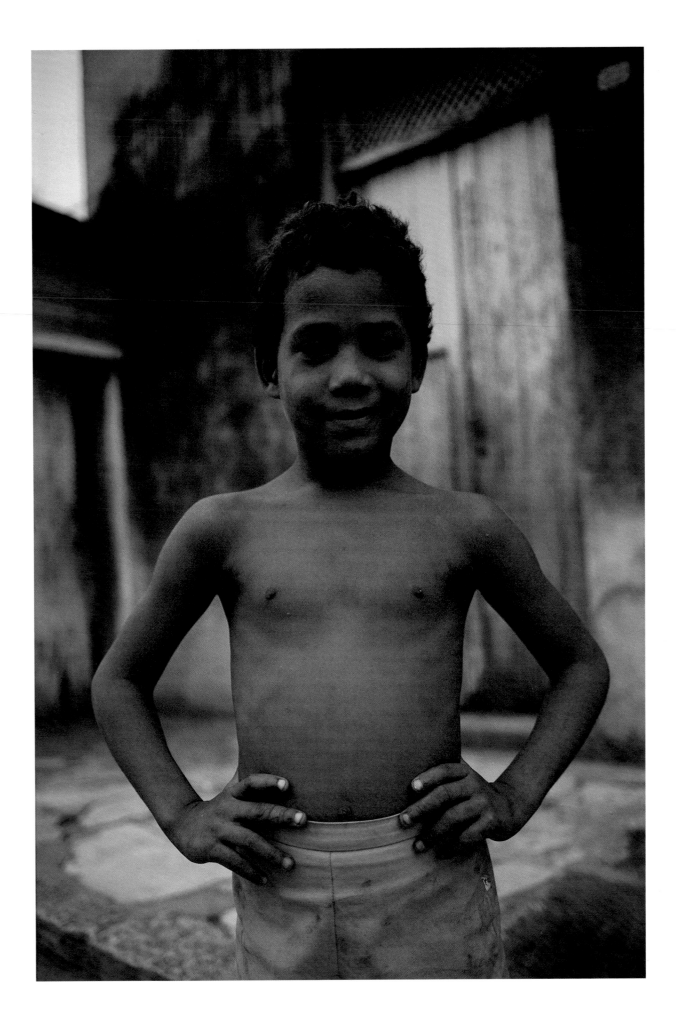

Portrait of
Cuba

GATHERING CANE

Early Cuba

CUBAN CHILDREN WITH FAMILY PIG.
ISLE OF PINES, CUBA. 1898.

The Ever
Faithful
Isle

Columbus landed in Cuba on his first voyage to the New World and proclaimed it the fairest land human eyes had ever seen. Many since have agreed with him. Cuba is indeed a beautiful island. Its soaring green mountains, gently rolling hills, and stately palms that rustle softly and eternally in the trade winds have a soothing quality to them. It is a landscape that seems to beckon and enfold. As one American expatriate put it years ago, "The soft beauty of this place puts my soul at rest."

For those who believe people are shaped by the land on which they live, the Cubans offer confirmatory evidence. The Siboné and Taino Indians who inhabited the island when

~

This photograph was taken as part of a study of Cuba and its people commissioned by the U.S. government shortly after it gained possession of the island.

Spanish nobleman

Diego de Velazquez

founded the first city

in Cuba, Baracoa,

in 1512. To the

disappointment of the

Spanish, there was

little gold in Cuba.

the Spanish arrived were peaceful, industrious, hospitable. The same may be said of the Cuban people today, grown out of the same soil over a period of four hundred years. They have a marked capacity to make the best of things and enjoy to the fullest whatever life has to offer. Certainly they laugh easier and dance with more abandon than almost anyone. Even today, the sheer joy on the faces of wildly gyrating couples at the *Tropicana* nightclub or in the humblest bar of the interior is testimony to the inextinguishable Cuban spirit, a *joie de vivre* with a frenetic mambo beat.

The Spanish who colonized the island were from a harsher soil. They were neither peaceful nor charitable, as the Indians soon learned. In 1512 a Spanish nobleman, Diego de Velazquez, founded the first city, Baracoa, near the site of Columbus's first landing at the eastern tip of the island. Within three years, the Spanish had established themselves from one end of the island to the other, seizing the land for themselves and enslaving the Indians. Of the Indian population of over 100,000 at the time the Spanish arrived, none survived the first half century of Spanish rule. Worked to death in the fields and mines, decimated by the diseases brought by the Europeans and often tortured and killed simply for sport, by 1570 the Indians were only a memory. Nothing of their culture remained but the names of a few geographic locations, including that of the island itself, Cuba.

For almost four centuries thereafter Cuba was a colony exploited by Spain and coveted by other powers, including the United States following its independence. To the disappointment of the Spanish, there proved to be little gold in Cuba. But the soil was fertile, almost incredibly so, and Cuba quickly became an important producer of tobacco, cattle and timber. Slaves were brought in from Africa to replace the lost Indian work force. After sugar became the mainstay of the Cuban economy in the 19th century, the number of slaves shot up from about 40,000 in 1774 to 470,000 in 1840 out of a total population of more than one million. By then Cuba accounted for almost one-third of world sugar production. Sugar had become king. It remains so today.

Lying as it does less than one hundred miles off the coast of Florida and directly athwart the entrance to the Gulf of Mexico, Cuba has been of marked strategic interest to the United States since the early days of the Republic. With the Louisiana Purchase of 1803, the Mississippi River became the American interior's outlet to the world through the port of New Orleans and the Gulf of Mexico. Thus it became a dictum of U.S. statesmen that Cuba must never fall into the hands of a powerful foe. The most certain way to prevent that was to add Cuba to the Union itself. From Thomas Jefferson on, American presidents held to that notion as an enduring goal. Jefferson tried to purchase Cuba from Spain in 1808. In 1823, he wrote, "I have ever looked on Cuba as the most interesting addition which could ever be made to our system of states….The control which…this island would give us over the Gulf of Mexico, and the countries of the isthmus bordering on it… would fill up the measure of our political well-being."

In that same year, John Quincy Adams described Cuba as a ripening fruit that would inevitably fall into the lap of the Union. Its importance to our national interests, he asserted, was greater than that of any other foreign territory. During the 19th century, four other American presidents tried to buy Cuba outright. There were also a number of abortive, and certainly less straightforward, schemes to transfer the island to American ownership.✳ In addition, there were three major filibustering expeditions. One of these, led by a Venezuelan-born former Spanish army officer named Narciso Lopez, came in 1850 and in many ways was a preview of the Bay of Pigs disaster more than a century later. Lopez had convinced a

Enslaved by the Spanish to work in fields and mines, the Sibonéy and Taino Indians did not survive the first half-century of Spanish rule.

✳ In 1854, for example, the American minister in Madrid, without authorization from Washington, tried to talk the Spanish government into negotiating a large loan from the United States to pay off other loans on which it was defaulting. Cuba was to be the collateral. The minister was certain the Spanish would default on this loan as well, leaving the U.S. in possession of Cuba. Unfortunately for the minister, the Spanish saw no reason not to continue with the first default and rejected his offer of a loan.

Slaves were brought from Africa to replace lost Indian labor. Incredibly fertile soil quickly made Cuba an important exporter of tobacco, cattle and timber.

number of American backers that the island was ready for revolt. With the tiniest spark, the Cubans would rise against their Spanish masters. Once free of Spain, he insinuated, they would of course rush to join the Union. Lopez tried to provide the spark by landing in the port of Cárdenas with more than five hundred men, most of them Mississippians and Kentuckians who spoke not a word of Spanish. Lopez spoke almost no English, nor did his Hungarian chief of staff, General Pragay. All orders had to be translated, sometimes several times. The command structure was described by the historian Edward S. Wallace as "…a sort of miniature but mobile Tower of Babel."

Whatever views Cubans may have had of the Spanish, they wanted nothing to do with this confused band of wild-eyed Americans who milled about in the city square, firing their rifles in the air and letting out exultant cries of victory. Rather than joyously welcoming the invaders as Lopez had predicted, the townspeople barricaded themselves in their homes and sent for help. A Spanish column was soon on the way and the invaders were forced to retreat to their boat, a side-wheeler named the *Creole*, and race for Key West, closely pursued by Spanish warships.

The next year Lopez was back again. This time his scheme ended in disaster. Lopez and four hundred Americans he talked into accompanying him were captured and many were executed. Among those who faced the firing squads was Colonel William L. Crittenden, a West Point graduate and the nephew of the governor of Kentucky. Tempers were high in New Orleans, from whence the expedition sailed, as word of the executions spread. U.S. newspapers, perhaps with a bit of embellishment, reported that upon being ordered to kneel and don a blindfold, Crittenden had shouted in a clear, fearless voice, "A Kentuckian kneels to none except his God, and always dies facing his enemy."

With Crittenden's connections and such reported histrionics as these, tempers were raised to a fevered pitch in the South. The fact that American blood had been shed, screamed the *Louisiana Courier*, "cries aloud for vengeance...blood for blood! Our brethren must be avenged! Cuba must be seized!"

But no further expeditions sailed, perhaps because of the fate that met the last one, or perhaps because the U.S. Government decided to discourage them.

It should be emphasized that the United States's obsession lay in acquiring the island, or at the very least, in making certain it did not pass from the hands of a weak Spain to those of a more formidable foe. American statesmen had no interest in seeing Cuba become independent. On the contrary, Cuban independence was regarded as something to be discouraged by every means available. American leaders tended to regard the Cuban population as a mongrel lot incapable of self-government. They feared that if the island gained independence, it would become a black republic, an event that could have unwanted consequences in the slave-holding states of the American South.

The other Spanish colonies in Latin America had won their independence by 1825, leaving Cuba and Puerto Rico as the last vestiges of what had been Madrid's vast empire in the New World. The Spanish began to call Cuba "The Ever Faithful Isle." But it was a misnomer, for more and more Cubans also wished to be free of Spanish rule. On October 10, 1868, the first of Cuba's wars for independence began when Carlos Manuel de Céspedes, a wealthy planter from Oriente province, freed his slaves, called for gradual emancipation throughout Cuba and proclaimed its independence. De Céspedes began with only thirty-seven men, but soon had thousands. The war raged on for a decade, matching Spain's well-armed regiments against rag-tag Cuban guerrilla fighters who knew the countryside far better than the Spanish. By 1878, the war having cost at least 200,000 lives and staggering property losses, both sides were exhausted. The Spanish offered an armistice, the Treaty of Zanjón. As it offered peace but not independence, many of the revolutionary generals refused to sign. Others did, but fighting broke out again in 1879, only to be put down quickly by fresh Spanish troops. What became clear was that the Ten Years War had sealed in blood the Cubans' determination to be free.

In accordance with its belief that Cuba ought not be independent, the United States did not extend belligerent rights to the insurgents or in any other way encourage them during the Ten Years War. Quite the contrary, President Grant's Secretary of State, Hamilton Fish Armstrong, made clear his low regard for the competence of the Cubans. A population consisting of Indians, Africans and Spaniards was obviously incapable of self-government, he believed. What the United States had hoped was that Spain would grow tired of the struggle and agree to a new American offer to buy Cuba. Though those hopes were dashed by the Treaty of Zanjón, American leaders knew they would have another opportunity.

The decade of 1880–90 saw dramatic changes in Cuba. Slavery had been abolished in 1868, and American investments began to surge into the island, by 1898 totalling close to $100 million, mostly into the sugar industry. Huge sugar centrals began to replace smaller mills.

With American backing, Narciso Lopez led two ill-fated expeditions to Cuba, 1850 and 1851, in the hope of forcing the Spanish from Cuba and bringing the island into the Union.

Sugar became the mainstay of the Cuban economy in the 19th Century. By 1840, the number of slaves brought in to work the cane fields had shot up to 470,000 out of a total population of one million.

Inexorably, a new war of independence began in 1895, this time led by José Martí, regarded as the heart and soul of Cuban independence. Martí, a student and poet of some local fame, was first imprisoned by the Spanish authorities in 1870. He moved to the United States in 1887 to begin organizing a new revolutionary party with the purpose of launching a final war of liberation. To support himself during his years in the United States, Martí worked as a correspondent for a number of important Latin American newspapers, covering among other things the first Pan American meeting in Washington in 1889. Wherever he was and whatever he was doing, poetry and essays flowed from the man, eventually filling more than seventy volumes. Martí is revered in Cuba not only as the man who

finally brought Cuba its independence, but also as the country's greatest man of letters.

In 1895, supported by a number of the revolutionary generals from the Ten Years War, such as the black general Antonio Maceo, called "the Bronze Titan," and the venerable Máximo Gomez, Martí landed in Oriente province to renew the struggle. An idealist, who dreamed not only of Cuba's independence but of a redemptive revolution to bring equal opportunity to all Cubans, he wrote in 1878, "Exclusive wealth is unjust.... A nation with small landowners is rich. A country with a few rich men is not rich.... In political economy and good government, distribution is the source of prosperity." Martí also insisted on the brotherhood of

Poet, statesman and

revolutionary hero —

José Martí dreamed of

a redemptive revolution

that would bring

economic and political

equality to all Cubans.

Martí is regarded as

the father of Cuban

independence.

black and white, arguing that those who wished to divide one from the other did a grave disservice to the revolution.

Therefore, this war of independence differed from earlier conflicts. As presented by Martí, it was a struggle not only for self-government, but also for social justice, racial equality and the economic well-being of all Cubans. As the historian Louis Pérez said so well, "Martí transformed rebellion into revolution."

Martí believed U.S. economic domination of Cuba would be as prejudicial to the island as Spanish political control had been. He warned his fellow Latin Americans to beware of growing U.S. insistence on Manifest Destiny, the belief that the American flag should fly from the Bering Straits to Tierra del Fuego.

Tragically, Martí was killed in one of the first battles of the new war, leaving the revolution without a political leader of stature. The military campaign ground on successfully, however, and by 1897, a new Spanish government was ready to make the first concession toward independence. Cuba was to become autonomous and elect its own government, though sovereignty would continue to reside with Spain. For the revolutionary generals, however, autonomy was not enough. The fight would go on until total independence was achieved. Spain was in fact exhausted and beaten, and the autonomy policy had backfired. No sooner was the first autonomous government installed in January of 1898 than native Spaniards in Cuba rioted. The new government was rejected as fiercely by the so-called Spanish volunteers as by the Cuban revolutionary forces. Pressure grew in Spain for total withdrawal and recognition of Cuban independence.

Full independence was not the outcome wished for by the United States. American investors in Cuba were made nervous by Martí's distributive rhetoric. They, along with many Cuban property owners, urged U.S. intervention, ostensibly to halt the bloodshed, but with the broader intention of blocking from power what they regarded as a radical revolutionary crowd. However, the revolutionary leaders understood the implications of U.S. intervention and opposed it. As the wary old Máximo Gomez put it, "[the] North American Republic's absorbing tendency" might overwhelm the cause of a truly independent Cuba. "Cuba must not be," he warned, "beholden for its independence in any way to foreign good graces."

Most Americans probably believe that had it not been for the Spanish-American War, Cuba would have remained a Spanish colony. American history texts for years asserted that the United States generously gave Cuba its independence after defeating the Spanish. The historical record supports the Cuban nationalists' far different view, which is that the successful conclusion of the long struggle for independence was almost at hand. Within a year at most, Spain would have been forced to withdraw from the "Ever Faithful Isle," leaving behind a sovereign Cuban nation.

It was at this point that the United States decided to step in. Still opposed to a fully independent Cuba, Washington wished to have some degree of control and had the support of many Cuban property owners.

After coveting the island for almost a century, the moment seemed at hand for the United States simply to take the island, and many U.S. leaders wished to do precisely that. However, the issue was clouded by the hysteria whipped up in the United States by William Randolph Hearst and other leaders of the yellow press. Wanting a "splendid little war" to demonstrate America's new power in the world –

José Martí

Heart & Soul of Cuban Independence

Almost a century after his death, José Martí remains the spiritual cornerstone of the Cuban identity, communist and non-communist. Known as the *Apóstol* (Apostle), Martí devoted his life to the struggle for an independent Cuba. His many volumes of poetry and prose championed the cause of the common people in Cuba and the rest of Latin America, calling for social, racial and economic equality for all.

Born in Havana in 1853, José Martí's political awareness materialized at an early age. At sixteen Martí published a newspaper, *La Patria Libré* (*The Free Fatherland*). In 1869, he was charged with treason by a Spanish court and sentenced to six months of hard labor at a stone quarry in Havana known as San Lázaro. Released from prison and exiled to Spain at age seventeen, Martí emerged from San Lázaro a man determined to lead his country to independence. In 1878 Martí returned to Cuba after general amnesty was granted to political prisoners and immediately resumed his revolutionary activities. Again, he was arrested for conspiracy and deported to Spain. Martí quickly left Spain and joined other Cuban exiles in New York to organize opposition to Spanish colonial rule. The Cuban Revolutionary party was formed in 1892 with Martí as president and General Máximo Gomez supreme commander of revolutionary forces. On April 11, 1895, Martí, Gomez and a band of followers landed on the south coast of Cuba to begin their armed struggle against the Spanish. Tragically, Martí was killed in a battle with the Spanish army in Oriente province on May 19, 1895, seven years before his dream of an independent Cuba was realized.

Ironically, the memory of Martí has been exploited by both sides of the current political standoff. Marxist Cubans hail Martí as the ideological architect of their communist revolution. Radio Martí and TV Martí broadcast anti-Castro rhetoric from South Florida with the support of Cuban exiles in Miami. Martí's popularity and importance to *all* Cubans testifies to his extraordinary vision.

and to raise circulation of their newspapers – Hearst and a number of other publishers printed stories of hideous atrocities committed by the Spanish troops in Cuba. If one went by the Hearst newspapers, blood ran two feet deep in every Cuban street and bloodthirsty Spaniards raped Cuban women on every block. As the Cuban people were cast in the role of victim, sympathy for them grew among the American people. This sympathy soon resulted in grassroots pressure to assist these people who were fighting for their independence the same way Americans had fought for theirs. Congress quickly caught the *Cuba Libré* mood, and public passions were further inflamed on February 15, 1898, by the destruction of the USS *Maine* in Havana Harbor. Because of the rioting on the part of Spanish citizens who opposed the idea of an autonomous Cuba, the American consul in Havana, Fitzhugh Lee of Civil War fame, had requested that a battleship be sent to make clear that American property and citizens had best be left alone. The *Maine* had been flying the flag in Havana Harbor three weeks when it was ripped apart by an explosion with a loss of 260 lives.

Predictably, the Hearst papers said the ship had been destroyed by a Spanish mine and demanded revenge. "Remember the *Maine*" became the battle cry of American troops in the war that followed. In fact, there was no Spanish mine. After a thorough investigation of all evidence, Admiral Hyman Rickover concluded in 1976 that the explosion almost certainly came from within the ship, probably the result of coal dust, a common danger in those days. The Spanish, of course, had the most to lose by blowing up the *Maine*. They knew full well what the reaction in the United States was likely to be. At the time, however, the truth mattered not at all. There was a national outcry in the United States. The public and Congress demanded war against Spain in favor of Cuban independence. On March 9, Congress voted to appropriate $50 million for war preparations. The McKinley Administration had to act before pressures reached such a critical mass that the restless Congress declared war on its own. The instinctive reaction was again to try to buy the island outright. As the American minister in Madrid told the Spanish minister of colonies, "The Spanish flag cannot give peace. There is but one power and one flag that can compel peace. That power is the United States and that flag is our flag."

Ultimately the Spanish could not bring themselves to accept the humiliation of selling the island under such circumstances. With their demurral, American armed intervention became inevitable. However, the McKinley Administration could not state that its goal was the acquisition of Cuba. Public opinion demanded *Cuba Libré*, and Congress echoed the call. The administration thus accepted a compromise. As the declaration of hostilities went forward, it carried an amendment added by Senator Henry M. Teller of Colorado under which the United States disclaimed any intention of exercising sovereignty over the island. The declared objectives were to restore the peace and then to leave the government of the island in the hands of the Cuban people. These were encouraging words to the Cuban revolutionaries who had warned that, without such a declaration of intent, they would fight the American army with the same determination they had showed against the Spanish.

The "yellow press" demanded revenge for the sinking of the USS Maine by the Spanish. It was later proven that the ship was a victim of a coal dust explosion.

Suspicious Cuban revolutionary leaders did note that the amendment would not prevent the United States from imposing a protectorate status on Cuba, even though the new government might be elected by the Cuban people. Ominously Washington still refused to recognize the Cuban revolutionaries "as an army or a people or a government."

Nor did the Teller Amendment settle the question of Cuba's future status for Americans. An overwhelming majority of the American public favored a free Cuba, as did most members of Congress. However, there were those in the McKinley

Administration and a sizable number of American business and military leaders who continued to believe that, after the fighting was over, Cubans would wish for or could be persuaded to ask for annexation. Meanwhile, the Teller Amendment was broad enough to assure de facto control of the island, which was the basic intent of the McKinley Administration.

And so on April 25, 1898, the United States declared war on Spain. The Spanish-American War would last just over three months and leave the U.S. in

The USS **Maine** *resting on the bottom of Havana Harbor, 1898.*

possession of Puerto Rico, the Philippines and Guam, as well as in control of Cuba.

There was never any doubt as to the outcome of the war. The Spanish fleet was no match for the American, and for all practical purposes the Spanish army had already been beaten in the field by the Cubans. The Spanish forces might as well have surrendered on April 25. However, wishing to save their honor, they braced for the onslaught. By the end of May, American ships had taken up stations off Santiago de Cuba, bottling up the Spanish squadron under the command of Admiral Cervera. On June 22, the American expeditionary force disembarked at Sibonéy, to the east of Santiago, and began to advance on the city.

The Battle of San Juan Hill, the only major land engagement of the war, was fought on July 1. The U.S. press blew the exploit out of proportion, describing it as one of the most heroic battles of all times. Theodore Roosevelt was said to have led the charge of his Rough Rider regiment astride a fierce stallion, his chest bared to enemy bullets, his sword flashing defiance. Such hyperbole aside, American troops did fight bravely and well that day, sustaining more than 1,500 casualties – 10% of the entire expeditionary force. Even if afoot rather than on a white horse, Roosevelt did participate in the charge, facing death as he did so.

"Remember the **Maine***"*

became the battle cry

of U.S. troops as they

charged San Juan Hill

on July 1, 1898.

Two days later, the Spanish fleet sailed out of Santiago Harbor in a vain effort to break through the American blockade. The running naval battle lasted several hours, but by the end of the day Cervera's fleet was at the bottom of the Caribbean.

Meanwhile, relations between the Americans and their Cuban allies deteriorated virtually to the breaking point. At first sight of the ragged Cuban forces, who had been fighting for three years under the most difficult conditions, the Americans decided they were worthless. Theodore Roosevelt described them as "a crew of as utter tatterdemalions as human eyes ever looked on…[who] would be of no use in serious fighting." The famous journalist and author Stephen Crane called them "half-starving ragamuffins," and "a collection of real tropic savages."

There was a good deal of racism behind these American attitudes. Many of the Cuban officers and soldiers were Negro or mulatto, a fact which simply confirmed the view of the Americans that Cubans would be incapable of self-government. "The valiant Cuban!" one American officer was reported to have remarked scornfully. "He strikes you first by his color. It ranges from chocolate yellow through all the shades to deepest black with kinky hair."

The Americans later complained that the Cuban people had given them little help and that they had not participated in the fighting. It could hardly have been otherwise, for the American command refused even to recognize the Cuban army. Before embarking for Cuba, they had agreed that the Cubans would be assigned to auxiliary tasks only, such as rear guard detail, trench digging and road building. General Calixto García, who commanded Cuban forces in the Santiago area, refused to assign his men to such tasks, insisting that they were "soldiers, not laborers."

Cooperation between the two armies was thus excluded. The Cubans were denied a front-line role by the American command and rejected the menial tasks in the rear assigned to them by the Americans. General García was outraged. But there was worse to come.

On July 17, the Spanish garrison in Santiago surrendered. For all practical purposes, the war was over. A few days later, American troops staged a victory parade through the streets of Santiago. Cuban troops were not invited to participate. In fact, García learned to his anger and consternation that the American commander, General William R. Shafter – jokingly said to have won the job on the basis of being the fattest man in the U.S. Army – had expressly forbidden Cuban forces from entering the city. This was to be portrayed as an American victory, not one in which the Cubans shared.

It is difficult for Americans to imagine how deeply this affront, and hundreds like it, was felt by the Cubans. Resentments smoldered for more than sixty years, particularly in the mind of a new Cuban revolutionary leader in 1959. As he entered Santiago in January of that year, Fidel Castro pointedly noted, "there is no General Shafter here now to prevent our victory march."

Immortalized for his heroics by the American press, Teddy Roosevelt rode his wartime popularity to the U.S. presidency in 1901.

84959

Spanish prisoners captured by U.S. forces kneel at the Arsenal, Santiago de Cuba, 1989.

THE VICTORIOUS
ROUGH RIDERS

Flush with victory,

Teddy Roosevelt's

Rough Rider regiment

poses for a victory

portrait atop San

Juan Hill.

On August 12, 1898, the United States and Spain formally signed an armistice. The war was officially over. As Cuban revolutionary leaders began to ask publicly if their struggle had been betrayed, the Americans moved to occupy the island and set up a military government. Almost four years of U.S. rule followed. The American occupiers clearly favored annexation. To General Leonard Wood, the American military governor, his job was to americanize the island so that Cubans would demand entry into the Union. Most wealthy planters and U.S. investors in Cuba were willing enough, but the majority of public opinion was not to be swayed. The Cuban people by and large backed the aging revolutionary generals in demanding independence. Thus, the Americans reluctantly began preparations to withdraw. The Cubans would have self-government. Ostensibly, Cuba would be an independent country. Full sovereignty was to be denied, however, for the United States was still determined to control the island. The instrument of that control was the so-called Platt Amendment, introduced by Senator Orville Platt of Washington in February of 1901. According to one of its provisions, the U.S. could intervene whenever it wished in order to protect life and property and to assure Cuban independence. Cubans were bitterly amused by this proviso, since the only

power threatening Cuban independence was the United States.

In effect, the amendment also gave the United States the right to review and approve all treaties between Cuba and third countries and any loans the Cubans might wish to contract with third parties. Finally, Cuba was required to sell or lease coaling or naval stations to the United States.

The Cuban public was outraged. There were demonstrations all over the island against the amendment. Encouraged by these events, delegates to the constitutional convention meeting in Havana indicated their intention to reject it. Washington was furious. "These people are base ingrates," said one American official. General Wood urged Washington to consider dissolving the convention. In the end, however, that proved unnecessary. U.S. representatives were simply instructed to inform the delegates that they had two options. They could accept the Platt Amendment as an appendix to the Cuban Constitution, or they could forget about U.S. withdrawal. American military occupation would continue indefinitely.

Sadly and reluctantly, on June 12, the convention accepted the inevitable by a vote of sixteen to eleven with four abstentions. "It is not the Republic we fought for...nor the absolute independence we dreamed of," brooded the embittered old

Cuban soldiers paved the way for the U.S. victory in Cuba, but American commanders denied them a front-line role in the Spanish-American War.

general-in-chief Máximo Gomez. But he urged his fellow countrymen to accept it as the lesser of two evils. Continued American occupation, he warned, would eventually result in the total americanization of the island. It was better to accept limited sovereignty and be rid of the Americans. Perhaps in the future, the dream of the Republic might be realized. Meanwhile, he concluded, "we must make great efforts always to remain Cubans."

With a protectorate status thus imposed on Cuba, the United States pulled down its flag on May 20, 1902. U.S. military occupation was at an end. The newly elected Cuban authorities, headed by President Estrada Palma, took over the reins of government. But U.S. impositions were only beginning. The U.S. immediately demanded and got a reciprocal trade agreement with the new Cuban state, an agreement that Cubans felt clearly favored American interests. "This is not a treaty of reciprocity," cried one Cuban senator. "The United States has simply replaced our old mother country…converting Cuba into a mercantile colony and the United States into the mother country."

A Cuban soldier proudly displays the flag of Cuba's newly won independence from almost four hundred years of Spanish colonial rule.

The thirty-one years that followed can be described as the period of the full protectorate. They were characterized by corrupt Cuban governments, which did what Washington demanded, and by growing U.S. financial interests in Cuba. American investments in Cuba increased almost eightfold between the end of U.S. military occupation and the beginning of the world depression. By 1929, the total reached more than $1.5 billion, almost 30% of American investments in all of Latin America. More striking, while American-owned sugar mills accounted for only 15% of Cuban production in 1906, by 1920 they accounted for almost 50%, and by 1929 for a staggering 75%. Clearly, American interests had come to dominate the Cuban economy. Though the percentage of U.S. investments and share of the Cuban sugar harvest declined somewhat after 1929, the latter never dropped below 40%.

These years were also characterized by the landing of U.S. Marines in various parts of the island to protect growing U.S. economic interests, and by a second U.S. occupation (1906–9) following a disputed election.

A quick boat ride from Florida, Havana became a playground for American tourists, a trend helped along by Prohibition in the United States. As one comedian commented at the time, "It was smart of us to give Cuba back to the Cubans. That way, we can still buy booze there." Spending a few days in Havana now became the thing to do, and there was no question as to the purpose: to sample the wildest night life in the Western Hemisphere. Casinos, night clubs, bars and brothels operated at maximum capacity. American tourists returned exhausted, describing Cuba as a "non-stop dance."

But the dancing slowed as the world depression hit in 1929. Gerardo Machado, president since 1925, had made himself the island's virtual dictator and carried corruption to new heights. Opposition to the already unpopular president grew as

Cuban General Calixto García (above) claimed his men were "soldiers, not laborers." He rejected the menial tasks assigned to them by U.S. commanders. General William Shafter (bottom, left) refused to recognize the Cuban army as a legitimate fighting force.

economic conditions worsened. Following widespread strikes and rioting, Machado was forced to resign on August 12, 1933. Appropriately, he flew into exile carrying five revolvers and several bags of gold.

A new period began in Cuban history and in relations between the United States and Cuba. Carlos Manuel de Céspedes was named acting president, but in fact Cuba was left without an effective government. Chaos reigned. Then, in September, in the midst of this volatile mess, an extraordinary thing happened. An army sergeant named Fulgencio Batista led a revolt of non-coms against their officers. Most active duty officers were cashiered, with the non-coms replacing them. Within a week, Sergeant Batista became Colonel Batista. With the army behind him, and after seeming to change sides several times, Batista threw his support to Dr. Ramón Grau San Martín, a politician who promised a more progressive but effective government. De Céspedes was forced to resign.

Grau, however, was not acceptable to the administration of newly inaugurated President Franklin D. Roosevelt. He was regarded as being too far to the left, and some of the people around him were accused of being communists. As proof of the "communistic tendencies" of the Grau government, U.S. Ambassador Jefferson Caffery pointed to the Workman's Compensation Law proposed by Grau and to a series of decrees affecting electricity rates (the electric power company belonged to U.S. interests). Ironically, the Cuban Communist Party was at the same time accusing Grau of being a "tool of the imperialists."

Irony aside, Washington flatly refused to accept the Grau government. Sumner Welles, Roosevelt's special emissary, made it clear the decision would not change regardless of how long Grau sat in the president's chair. Cuban nationalists were delighted. As one of them stated, "at last we have a president who isn't controlled by the American Embassy."

Cuban nationalists were pleased, but Colonel Batista was not. He wanted no confrontation with the United States, and by then he was the real power in Cuba. In January of 1934, Grau was forced out and was soon replaced by

LOADS OF SUGAR CANE BEING
BROUGHT TO THE SUGAR MILLS. 1900.

Colonel Carlos Mendieta, a Batista appointee. United States recognition soon followed. The Batista Era had begun. Until 1940, through a series of puppet presidents, Batista ruled from behind the scenes as the strongman of Cuba. Though an iron-fisted ruler, he was not unpopular. In 1940 he became president in open and reasonably free elections, with a term running to 1944. As Cuban nationalists saw it, the United States had again acted to deny Cuba full sovereignty and to prevent the sort of redemptive revolution Martí had envisioned forty years before.

This judgment may have been unfair. Leaving aside the question of his alleged "leftism," the fact was that Grau's government did not succeed in restoring stability or in rallying a strong coalition of forces around it. Whether Grau would have presided over a redemptive revolution had he been left in power is open to serious question. When Grau was later elected president in 1944, he led an avalanche of corruption, not a revolution. Justified or not, a whole new revolutionary generation determined to break free of U.S. control. Fidel Castro was part of that generation. Says the British historian Hugh Thomas, "The revolution of 1959 followed in the wake of that of 1933 as the Second World War followed the First, or the revolution in Russia in 1917 that of 1905."

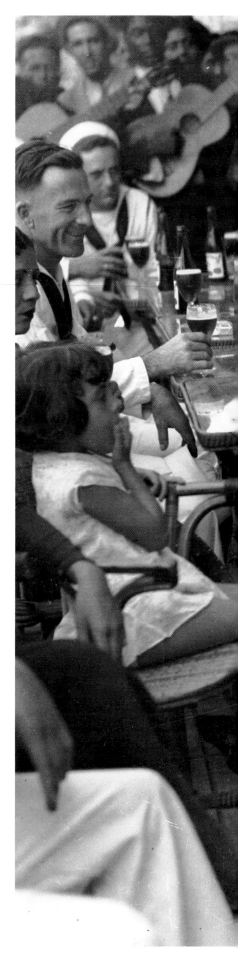

U.S. sailors at Sloppy Joe's, Havana in the twenties. Cuba became a playground for Americans wishing to escape the moral confines of Prohibition.

If the Roosevelt Administration helped bring about the Batista era and set in motion events leading to U.S.-Cuban confrontation in the sixties, it also immediately brought forth a new and more equitable look to U.S.-Cuban relations. The period of the full protectorate came to an end. In 1934, the United States abrogated the Platt Amendment. American warships might still lie in Havana Harbor, but they no longer had any treaty right to land their marines. This was the beginning of Roosevelt's Good Neighbor Policy. Interventions were now considered to be in bad form. At the 1933 Pan American Conference, the United States accepted a resolution that called on all the nations of the hemisphere to refrain from intervening in the affairs of their neighbors. Although the United States was not mentioned by name, there was no question as to where the resolution was aimed.

In 1903, exercising its rights under the Platt Amendment, the United States had acquired a naval base at Guantánamo Bay on the south coast of Cuba. With the abrogation of the amendment, a new base treaty was negotiated and signed in 1934. It should be added that this treaty did not run for ninety-nine years, as is commonly believed in the United States, but until abrogated or modified with the consent of both parties. In other words, unless the United States was willing to give it up, the American flag could fly over Guantánamo Bay forever. This arrangement was taken as an affront to national sovereignty by a growing number of Cubans in the years after 1934.

While the aims of Cuban nationalists and U.S. policymakers were inevitably antithetical, it had little impact on the relations between the Cuban and American people. On the contrary, Cubans and Americans got along famously on a personal

basis. They shared a similar sense of humor and easy-going styles. Cubans disapproved of certain U.S. policies, but there were many things about the American way of life they liked and even emulated. Baseball was, and is, the Cuban national sport, as it is the American. If anything, it is an even greater passion with Cubans. During the forties and fifties, the dream of even the most humble Cuban was to go to the United States to see a World Series. Havana had a team called the "Sugar Kings" in the American minor leagues during those years, and there were few major league teams in the United States that did not have Cuban players. Remember that Santiago, the central character in Ernest Hemingway's *The Old Man and the Sea*, dreamt of the great DiMaggio as he drifted through the Gulf Stream with a monster fish on the end of his line.

Hundreds of thousands of Cubans travelled to the United States, and tens of thousands lived there. Indeed, the Cuban colonies in Tampa and Key West date well back into the last century, and the flow was reciprocal. Swarms of Americans spent weekends in Cuba over the years, to dance, to gamble and have a good time, to belly up to the bar at Sloppy Joe's and to eat at the *Floridita* or *La Bodeguita del Medio*. Thousands of others worked and made their homes there. At the time of Castro's triumph in 1959, some 25,000 Americans resided in Havana alone.

Ernest Hemingway was one of them. It would be difficult to exaggerate his importance as a medium of mutual understanding. As he was lionized in the United States, so was he in Cuba. Cubans still revere him and his works. No

other literary figure is more read in Cuba, with the exception of José Martí himself. Yet, Hemingway sprang from the heartland of the feared and resented giant to the north. That made no difference. As one Cuban writer commented, "The Americans we read about in Hemingway's novels and short stories are people we can understand and for whom we can feel a deep affinity. Through Hemingway's eyes, we see a United States for which we can have a certain love, even as we resent some of her attitudes towards us."

That perhaps best sums up the Cuban attitude towards the United States; it is very much a love-hate relationship. That remained the case even after the triumph of Castro's revolution. A Cuban diplomat

Hero of the struggle against Spanish rule, General Calixto García Iniques (top). Carlos Mendieta (center) was appointed president by Batista following a coup in 1934. Ramone Grau San Martín (bottom) was elected president of Cuba in 1944.

phrased it well at the end of the seventies. "We continue to love you as people," he said, "even as we dislike your government's policies."

Despite continuing Cuban resentment of the dominating U.S. shadow, close ties developed between the two societies. It is probably fair to say that by 1959, no other country in the world, with the exception of Canada, quite so resembled the United States. At least that was true in the cities, with their department stores, five and dimes, supermarkets, ice cream parlors, American cars, TV shows and first-run American movies. Virtually every piece of machinery on the island was American-made. As the wife of an American businessman commented in 1958, "Except that everyone speaks Spanish, I wouldn't know I'd left the U.S. Oh sure, Havana has some old Spanish buildings, but then so do San Antonio and St. Augustine."

After serving a four-year term as the elected president, Fulgencio Batista allowed elections to be held in 1944. He had expected his hand-picked candidate, Carlos Saladrigas, to win. To the surprise of all, the election was won by the opposition candidate, none other than Grau San Martín, the very man Batista had deposed ten years earlier. Having miscalculated, Batista might have voided the elections and simply declared his candidate the winner. Many Cubans expected he would do precisely that. But he did not. Bowing to the will of the majority, Batista allowed the outcome to stand. He turned power over to Grau and went to live in retirement in Key Biscayne, Florida.

In retrospect, this was not an uncharacteristic decision on Batista's part. Military strongman and Machiavellian political maneuverer

though he was, Batista had not proved to be a reactionary despot during his first eleven years of control (1933–44). Quite the contrary, being a mulatto of most humble origins, he had quickly established himself as something of a populist. The United States had considered Grau to be too far to the left; yet, Batista managed to enact social and labor legislation that went beyond what Grau had advocated. Batista helped the Cuban labor movement become one of the most powerful and effective in the hemisphere. The Constitution of 1940, enacted during his stewardship, was among Latin America's most progressive. That Batista achieved these gains while maintaining good relations with the United States and actually broadening the parameters of Cuban independence was a tribute to his political

Gerardo Machado (top) was president of Cuba from 1925 until being forced from power in 1933. Tomás Estrada Palma (center) became the first president of independant Cuba in 1902. Carlos Prío Socarrás (bottom) was president from 1948–52.

*Interior of a cigar
factory in Havana,
circa 1900. The man
in the elevated seat in
the middle of the room
was employed to read
to the cigarmakers
while they worked,
an idea originated
by José Martí.*

skills. As he departed for Key Biscayne, Florida, Batista left behind a country that was more stable, more solvent and better prepared for democratic rule than when he had taken over. Had he remained in retirement, he would have been remembered well by history.

Moreover, had Batista's freely elected successor, Grau San Martín, governed honestly and conscientiously on the basis of the Constitution of 1940, democracy in Cuba might have been consolidated. Instead, during his four-year presidency, Grau indulged in an orgy of corruption, while at the same time ignoring the needs of the nation. That the treasury was not bankrupt by the end of his term was only because the sugar harvests had been so good and the world market prices so high that not even Grau could steal the money as fast as it came in. There had been a spirit of optimism in Cuba in 1944, a sense that the nation was at last on the way to the kind of government of which José Martí, Máximo Gomez and the other great revolutionary leaders had dreamed. Grau and his cronies dispelled the dream, or at least delayed it.

In the election of 1948, Grau was replaced by Carlos Prío Socarrás, one of his closest proteges from the *Autentico* party. Prío proved as venal and irresponsible as Grau himself. It is fair to say that these two did more to cast doubt on the efficacy of the democratic system than any other figures in Cuban history. After their experience under Grau and Prío, many Cubans asked themselves if democratic processes were really what they wanted and needed.

It was with the Cuban people in such a frame of mind that Batista returned to power. New elections were to be held in June of 1952. Sensing that the Cuban people were sick of the *Autenticos*, Batista tossed his hat into the electoral ring. He thought it was time to come back from Key Biscayne. Again he had miscalculated. A new reform party, the *Ortodoxos*, had entered the race promising to clean up corruption and live by the Constitution of 1940. Three months before the election, the new party seemed on the way to victory, but this time Batista was not to be denied. In March, friends in the army staged a coup on his behalf, stating that they did so because of evidence that Prío was preparing to steal the elections. The army never explained why elections were not then held between Batista and the *Ortodoxos*.

To his everlasting shame, Prío made no effort whatsoever to resist. Though some garrisons, as well as students and common citizens, offered to fight for him, he simply boarded a plane for Miami, departing as disgracefully as he had ruled.

Most Cubans took the news with a mixture of relief and resignation. They remembered Batista as not having been so bad. Cubans had come to believe all governments were corrupt; perhaps Batista's would be less so. Certainly he could not be more ineffective than Grau and Prío. Even those who had expected an *Ortodoxo* victory consoled themselves with the fatalistic thought that once in power the *Ortodoxos* might have proved as great a disappointment as the *Autenticos*.

But if the great majority of Cubans were prepared to acquiesce to Batista's seizure of power, there was one who was not: Fidel Castro.

~

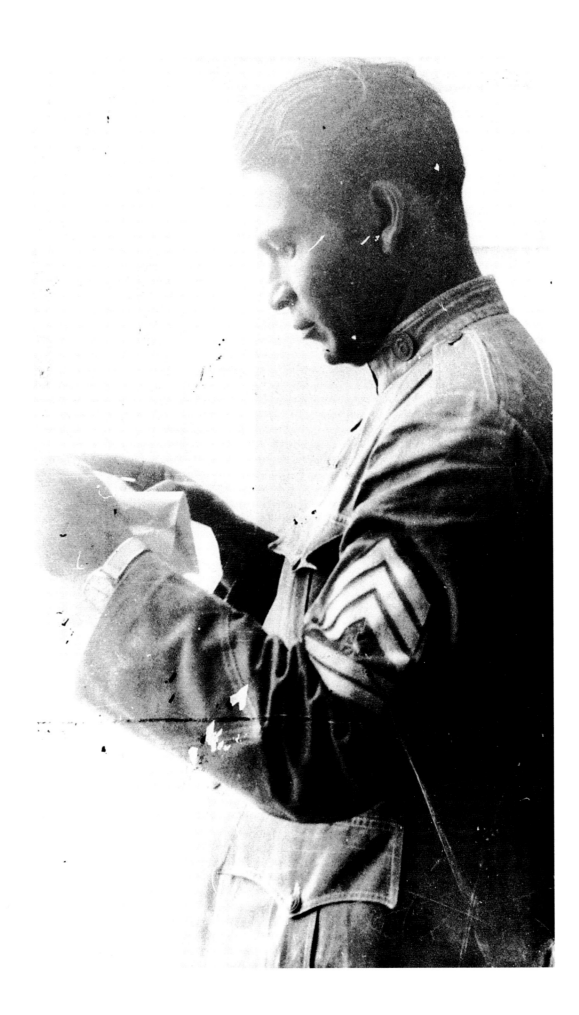

Enter Fidel

They Came From The Hills

newly practicing lawyer and member of the *Ortodoxo* party, Fidel Castro was a candidate for the Cuban House of Representatives in the election aborted by Batista's coup. He was running in a poor district of Havana where he was tremendously popular and almost certainly would have won. It is interesting to imagine how different Cuban history might have been had Batista remained in retirement in Key Biscayne and allowed the elections to go forward.

~

Fidel Castro in the mountains of the Sierra Maestra. These mountains were the ideal hideout from which to launch his attacks against dictator Fulgencio Batista.

The *Ortodoxos* most likely would have won the elections of June 1952 and begun a process of reform. Fidel Castro would have become a member of congress. With his political career launched, it is most likely that he would have gone on to win a senate seat, and finally run for the presidency itself. Politicians of his vision, determination and charismatic talents come along only rarely in any country. Chances are he would have become president of Cuba within a decade or so, but as the result of a democratic election rather than a revolution. Castro would have been bound by the Constitution of 1940, which the *Ortodoxos* would have restored had they come to office in June of 1952. Had he been elected to the presidency, Castro would most likely now be remembered as having been one of Cuba's most dynamic and effective democratic presidents – his term of office long ago having expired.

All speculating aside, the reality is that Batista did seize power, and that act launched Castro on a political career of a very different kind. Others accepted Batista's coup with weary resignation; not Castro. He vowed to force Batista from office and immediately set out to organize forces to do so. At first he tried working with the leaders of the established political parties, including his own *Ortodoxos*, to create a united front against Batista. However, they were unwilling to take a stand for fear of Batista's vengeful wrath. Castro quickly concluded that armed struggle was the only feasible course of action. He later extended this conclusion to Latin America as a whole. He secretly began gathering about him a small group of daring revolutionaries who would take up where Martí had left off. With his dash and reputation for action, he had little difficulty drawing such people to him. By July of the next year, he was ready to begin the struggle.

Leaving his young wife (they married in 1948) and four-year-old son behind in Havana, he moved his band to Oriente province, with headquarters at a farm just outside Santiago de Cuba. The plan for his opening attack was a daring one. Fidel and 123 of his followers were to attack the Moncada barracks in Santiago at dawn on July 26, then broadcast an appeal to the people of Cuba to rise in arms against the tyrant. Moncada was a major installation defended by more than four hundred of Batista's best troops. Castro counted on surprise, but fate was against him. Not all the attackers arrived in time and those who did ran into an unexpected patrol. The

Batista in New York, 1950, two years before he would return to power in his second coup.

element of surprise was lost. Forced to retreat under a hail of machine gun bullets, many of the attackers were killed outright or immediately taken prisoner, then tortured and killed. Castro and a few other survivors escaped to the hills, but were apprehended within days.

Colonel Alberto del Rio Chaviano, the commander at Moncada, had given orders that Castro was not to be arrested but shot on sight. Fortunately for Castro, the army platoon that cornered him was led by Lieutenant Pedro Manuel Sarría, a black officer who may have sympathized with Castro's cause. In any event, he ordered his men to hold their fire and allow Castro to give himself up. When Castro asked Sarría why he did not obey the order to kill him, the lieutenant replied he was not that kind of man.

"But if you spare me, they may kill you," Castro pointed out.

"Then let them kill me," Sarría said. "It is one's ethics that decide what one will do."

Sarría was not killed. He lived through the revolution and at its end was rewarded by Castro with command of his security detail.

The attack on Moncada was a military failure but a political success. It skyrocketed Castro to prominence. He added further to his image by defending himself at his trial with the kind of fiery and eloquent speech that was to become his trademark. A devastating statement of the ills and illegitimacy of the Batista government and the duty of patriots to stand against it, Castro's defense ended with the ringing words, "Condemn me if you will! History will absolve me!"

Rosa Lesdera protests

the death of her son

at the hands of

Batista's henchmen;

New York, 1957.

Mafia boss Santos

Trafficante (above,

center) controlled the

casinos and other mob

interests in Cuba.

A lotteryman (opposite),

Santiago de Cuba, 1959.

Castro had good material with which to work. He could hardly have exaggerated the sins of the Batista regime. If Batista had been considered a man of the people during his first period in power, he was a changed man when he returned from Key Biscayne. It has been suggested that he was ruined by inactivity and rich man's living. An energetic, dynamic leader in the thirties and forties, he now gave little attention to governing, preferring to spend long hours each day playing cards with friends or carousing by the pool at his country estate, Kuquine. Where he had once tried to expand Cuba's independence from the United States, the new Batista became a Cold War warrior to curry favor with Washington. During the Allied alliance against Germany in World War II, he had brought two members of the Communist party into his cabinet. Now, he outlawed the party and even established a Bureau for the Repression of Communism (BRAC), much to the delight of the John Foster Dulles State Department.

Although never above pocketing government money, after coming to power in 1952, Batista carried corrupt practices to the extremes of the Grau and Prío presidencies. Corruption under Batista took on a more sinister form as organized crime from the United States was sold an expanding piece of the action in Cuba. By 1957, American gangsters controlled most of the nightclubs and casinos and some of the major hotels in Havana, and they were moving into other business sectors as well.

Increasingly embarrassed by Batista's venality and tawdry conduct, Cubans were hoping for a champion who might restore national dignity. Fidel Castro's daring, if futile, attack on the Moncada barracks and his impassioned speech at the trial established him early as that champion, though he would have to wait before again taking sword in hand. For eloquent though his defense had been, Castro and his men were convicted and sentenced to long prison terms on the Isle of Pines.

The conditions of their confinement proved not too arduous. On the contrary, perhaps because they were such high-profile prisoners, they were relatively well treated. As Castro said later, he used prison as a postgraduate school, for he was allowed to bring in all the books he wished. "I devoured hundreds of books on politics, history and economics," he said. "If I hadn't read all I should in the university, I now had a chance to make up for it in prison. By the time I came out of prison, my education was complete."

By then he was also divorced. On her side, Mirta Castro must have had enough. She had married a man whose real life was revolution. Except for the idyllic first few months of their marriage, he had been so wrapped up in politics as to have little time for her or for their son, though it became clear in later life that Castro loved the boy deeply. For three years, she had hardly seen her husband at all. Nor could she expect things to change once he was out of prison. His letters to her spoke clearly of his determination to continue the struggle.

To the extent that Mirta was interested in politics, her views were incompatible with Fidel's. She was of the Diaz Balart family from Banes, in Oriente province. Close to Batista, who was also from Banes, her family liked neither the young Castro nor his politics. One can imagine the pressure they exerted on Mirta to divorce her radical "jailbird."

The divorce, in any case, was one of mutual consent. Fidel had been embarrassed by the revelation that his wife was on the payroll of the minister of interior, having been given a sinecure by one of her family members. Even so, Fidel and Mirta remained on reasonably good terms. She made arrangements for him to see his son, even during Fidel's period of self-imposed exile in Mexico. Castro has always remained in touch with his former wife who remarried and soon moved to Spain where she lives today. Once a year, she travels quietly to Cuba to visit her son, Fidelito, and her grandchildren.

As Castro was moving through his "postgraduate courses" on the Isle of Pines, his friends and political allies launched a campaign for his release. On May 6 of 1955, feeling not only magnanimous but totally secure in power, Batista did something he must have regretted for the rest of his life: he granted amnesty to Castro and all his men in honor of Mother's Day. If he expected their gratitude, or at least their silence, he was sharply disappointed. No sooner was Castro back on the mainland than he published a manifesto declaring that the war against Batista was just beginning. Surprisingly, Castro and his men were not returned to prison. Perhaps they would have been had they not soon departed for Mexico, where Castro decided they would go to prepare themselves for the guerrilla warfare that was to come. Much to Batista's chagrin, Castro left behind a message to the Cuban people which was given wide circulation by the popular Cuban magazine *Bohemia.*

> I am leaving Cuba because all doors of peaceful struggle have
> been closed....As a follower of Martí, I believe the hour has come
> to take rights and not beg for them, to fight instead of pleading
> for them. I will reside somewhere in the Caribbean. From trips
> such as this, one does not return or else one returns with the
> tyranny beheaded at one's feet.

The next seventeen months were crucial in Castro's odyssey. Living in safe houses and frequently dodging the Mexican police, he and more than one hundred companions – joined by the Argentine revolutionary Ernesto "Ché" Guevara – trained tirelessly in the Mexican countryside under the eye of Alberto Bayó, a famous old general of the Spanish Republican Army. Financed in large part by wealthy Cuban exiles living in Miami, including Prío Socarrás, Castro and his group bought a motor launch in Brownsville, Texas. Aboard the famous *Granma,* short for grandmother, they would return to Cuba to begin the fight anew. Amusingly, the official newspaper of the Cuban Communist party has been entitled *Granma* since 1965. Few Cubans are aware of its meaning in English, thus missing the irony.

Castro had vowed to return to the island before the end of 1956, and he was as good as his word. His homecoming, however, was a debacle. First of all, the *Granma* was only large enough to carry about eighty-five men, and even then it was badly overcrowded. As a result, Castro had to leave behind more than a third of his

Debutante Maria Delores Carillo at a Carnival ball, Havana, 1958. She typified the lifestyle of the few "haves" which differed drastically from the poverty of the "have-nots."

force. Worse, they encountered foul weather at sea, which delayed them two full days.

The plan had been to land on the southwest coast of Oriente province on November 30. At the same time the revolutionaries in Santiago de Cuba would stage an uprising to divert the army's attention. Unaware that the *Granma* was still two days to the east, the group in Santiago launched their attack and were bloodily repulsed. Their only effect was to alert the army that something was brewing. Word went out to be on the lookout for Castro's expedition. When Castro's group finally arrived on December 2, they were quickly spotted by government forces and brought under withering fire. To make matters worse, they had landed in the wrong place, a mangrove swamp rather than on the beach further down the coast. With the landing party quickly separated and hunted down by the army,

Tourists (opposite)

gamble at the Rivieria

Hotel in Havana, 1958.

Fidel Castro (above) in

exile in Mexico. He vowed

to return to Cuba with

"tyranny beheaded."

it appeared Castro's revolution might be over on the first day. In the confusion, Castro found himself alone in the middle of a cane field, soldiers on all sides. After a time he was joined by a second member of the group, Universo Sanchez, then later by Faustino Perez. As Tad Szulc relates the story in *Fidel: A Critical Portrait*, upon the appearance of Faustino, Castro was elated. It was as though a crucial turning point had been reached. "We are winning…. Victory will be ours!" he exulted. Universo Sanchez and Faustino Perez said nothing.

Sanchez and Perez doubtless admired their chief's unshakable confidence even in that dark moment, but as Szulc points out, so far as they knew, the three of them in the middle of that cane field surrounded by government troops might at that moment constitute the whole of the rebel army.

It was five days before the troops moved off and the three of them could emerge from their hiding place in the cane field. During those five days Castro kept their spirits up with his constant optimism. After eight more days, they encountered Fidel's younger brother Raúl and four other survivors. A few days later, Ché Guevara and six more turned up. Castro was ecstatic. From three men hiding in a cane field, he had a force of fourteen! If he had been confident in the cane field, his enthusiasm was now uncontainable.

Quickly the little band made its way into the Sierra Maestra mountains. Sheltered and aided by the peasants, they were able to regroup and begin the guerrilla campaign that a little more than two years later would result in Batista's downfall. The Batista government reported that Castro and his men had been killed and the rebellion snuffed out. The 26th of July Underground knew better; it was in contact with Castro and his newly established guerrilla front. But who would believe the underground's assurances that Castro was indeed alive? Cleverly, the underground contacted Herbert Matthews of *The New York Times* and smuggled him past Batista's troops and into the mountains. In February of 1957, Matthews interviewed Castro in his Sierra Maestra hideaway. No, Castro said, obviously he was not dead. On the contrary, his guerrilla army was on the march and the dictator's days were numbered. To give the impression that his "army" was

American Don Soldini

(above, upper right)

fought with Cuban rebels

to overthrow the Batista

regime. He was later

imprisoned by Castro.

Soldini (below, center)

dines with Castro before

leaving Cuba in 1959.

more numerous than it in fact was, Castro had the same men straggle in from different directions and speak of the need to contact other columns which were supposedly nearby. Matthews returned with word that Castro headed a formidable force.

From that point forward, the movement took off. Hundreds of youths from the cities and towns flocked to Castro's banner. An effective courier system brought the guerrillas supplies and communications from the 26th of July Underground in Santiago and Havana. Soon, they were able to broaden the field of combat. In mid-1957, Ché Guevara began operating in the central Sierra Maestra, around El Hombrito. Early the next year, Raúl led a column into the Sierra Cristal, a mountain range along the north coast of Oriente province, while Juan Almeida opened a third front in the eastern ranges of the Sierra Maestra, northwest of Santiago de Cuba. Another of the colorful commanders, Camilo Cienfuegos, first moved north toward Bayamo, then in the latter part of 1958 began moving up the island toward Havana.

The Castro-led rebellion captured the imagination not just of the Cubans, but of the world. It could not have been otherwise. The image of this brave band of dashing rebels, who were defeating the powerful Cuban army in the field and bringing the Batista dictatorship to its knees, inspired much admiration.

A number of idealistic young Americans were drawn to the fight. One was Don Soldini from New York, who at age nineteen joined the rebels in the mountains in early 1958. Soldini was wounded in the fighting and at one point captured and tortured by the dreaded Military Intelligence (SIM) before managing to escape. Now a successful businessman in Ft. Lauderdale, Soldini commented, "God, those days in the mountains were wonderful. Cuba was the most beautiful island in the world; the Cuban people were warm, generous and brave – and committed with a passion to the struggle against Batista. It was one of those moments of pure idealism, of pure romanticism. No matter what happened later, I wouldn't have missed those days alongside my comrades-in-arms for anything."

Castro's 26th of July group was not the only one to take up arms. An underground movement of students called the *Directorio Revolucionario* (the Revolutionary Directorate) carried out sabotage operations and hit-and-run raids in the cities. On March 13, 1957, they attacked the Presidential Palace itself. The objective was to kill Batista, but they failed. He was on the top floor, which

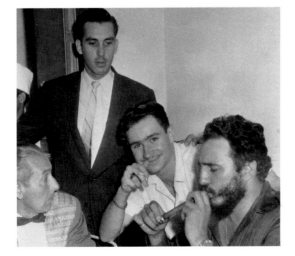

unbeknownst to the attackers could only be reached by an elevator that had been turned off as soon as the attack began. The attackers died courageously but hopelessly at the entrance to the palace, trying to force their way up the stairs. Nearby, their leader José Antonio Echevarría was killed as a support group shot it out with police. The *Directorio Revolucionario* remained active during the entire revolutionary struggle, but never recovered from the leadership losses of that fatal day.

In 1958, another group, the Second Front Escambray, led by a Spanish-born revolutionary, Eloy Gutierrez Menoyo, and William Morgan, a swashbuckling American former paratrooper, opened guerrilla operations in the Escambray Mountains of central Santa Clara province.

By mid-1958, Batista was indeed besieged. His eventual defeat, however, came about not because he faced a superior military force. The total number of guerrillas in the mountains never exceeded more than three thousand. Though the guerrillas were supported by thousands more working underground, Batista always had the advantage in terms of numbers and armaments. But while the guerrillas were fighting for a popular cause, led by charismatic figures who fought beside their men and shared their hardships, the Batista army was poorly commanded. Batista's officers often stole the pay of their soldiers, and certainly the senior officers never shared any hardships. Moreover, the army had no idea how to fight a guerrilla war. In late 1958, for example, in order to stop the rebels from advancing on Santa Clara, Batista's generals sent an armored train down the central railway line. Anchored to its tracks, the armored train was largely ineffective in fighting the highly mobile and

Fidel Castro instructs

rebel recruits in the

Cuban countryside.

Street fighting in

the cities erupted

between Castro

supporters and

Batista sympa-

thizers in the chaos

preceding Castro's

triumphant arrival

in Havana.

Camilo Cienfuegos was a colorful leader and Castro confidant during the revolution.

elusive guerrillas. An American Army attaché in Havana at the time simply shook his head. "With these tactics, the rebels will be in Havana within three months," he predicted quite accurately.

The common Cuban soldier became increasingly demoralized as he realized he was fighting for an unpopular cause and defending a dictator whose corrupt system was hated by the vast majority of Cubans. If Batista had retained any degree of popular support before December 1956, he quickly lost it by overreacting to the rebellion. His secret police arrested thousands of youths, tortured many and left bodies hanging on poles by the roadside as a warning to anyone who might be thinking of joining the opposition. These tactics backfired. The more repressive Batista became, the more intense was the hatred of his regime. By the end of 1958, it is fair to say that 95% of the Cuban population was in opposition to Batista, if only in spirit. By that point, Batista's soldiers would not fight anymore.

In addition to the armed rebel groups, there existed many civilian political organizations also demanding the dictator's resignation. However, little doubt remained as to who would dominate the political landscape after the revolution. Castro's pronouncements reflected his early association with the *Ortodoxo* party. His

various manifestoes spoke of restoring the Constitution of 1940, holding free elections and carrying out tax and land reforms. At one point, Castro said he had no intention of governing the country. He was a revolutionary and once the revolution was over he would leave the governing to others.

Did Castro ever really intend to fulfill these promises, to step aside, to hold elections, to restore the constitution? Probably not. After winning the revolution, elections and the Constitution of 1940 were simply relegated to the category of things that might be contemplated at a future point, "when the right conditions had been achieved." In fact, they were soon forgotten, never to be mentioned again. Castro did make a brief pretense of leaving the government in the hands of others. Manuel Urrútia, a Santiago judge who had tried to defend the rights of the Moncada prisoners, was appointed provisional president. José Miró Cardona, a prominent lawyer, was named prime minister. But it was always clear that Fidel was in command. Recognizing that fact, Miró Cardona resigned in February of 1959. Urrútia was forced out in July.

By the end of December 1958, Batista's government was in ruins. It was clear to everyone in Cuba that the end was only weeks away. As though to play a final joke

A young supporter

of the revolution

wearing a 26th of July

Movement armband.

on the country, Batista resigned and fled Cuba on New Year's Eve with his family, friends and ill-gotten wealth, leaving the island with an uncertain future as well as a hangover. Cubans who were still up at 5 am, or who had just arisen and turned on their radios, knew instantly the rebels had won. The music blaring out at them was *"Mamá, son de la loma"* ("Mama, they're from the hills"), the song of the 26th of July Movement, which had been played every night during the Revolution on a small clandestine transmitter called *Radio Rebelde* (Rebel Radio). As the song had been banned from other radio stations, the fact that it was being played meant only one thing: Batista had fled; the rebel army would soon be in Havana.

It was even sooner in Santiago. Castro entered the city the very next day on January 2, took possession of the Moncada barracks, where his revolution had begun, and spoke that night to an ecstatic crowd. He told them the *real* revolution – the struggle to build a new country with a just society – would now begin. This time, he went on, "...the Revolution will truly come to power. It will not be like 1898, when the North Americans came and made themselves masters of our country....For the first time the republic will be entirely free and the people will have what they deserve...."

It was not by chance that Castro referred back to 1898, or that he patterned himself after José Martí, or even that he at first promised to restore the Constitution of 1940. This was a nationalist revolution, and no one was better than Castro at utilizing the symbols and touching the well-springs of nationalism, or at reaching back into the past in order to explain and sanctify the decisions he was making in the present. If José Martí had warned against North American domination, Fidel Castro would now break that domination. If Martí had called for a redemptive revolution, Castro would now lead one.

As he marched into Havana in January of 1959, Castro was greeted as the greatest national hero since José Martí. Indeed, there was even a sign that he must have been sent by the gods. On January 8, as he was giving his first televised speech to the nation before a huge audience, one of the doves released as a symbol of peace suddenly returned from the sky and landed on his shoulder. It remained perched there during the entire speech, its eyes fixed on the mystified crowd. Shivers went up the spines of those watching. Who could now doubt it? Fidel was the anointed one. To the millions of Cubans who practiced or at least had a healthy respect for *Santería*, the worship of the old African gods, the sign was unmistakable. Doves are the messengers of Obatalá, the god who ranks just under the god of all creation. When the dove landed on Fidel's shoulder, it meant he had been chosen, or mounted, by the gods. He was *El Elegido* (the Chosen One), or *El Caballo* (the Horse). There was a collective gasp from the crowd, many falling to their knees. Even to those who ignored *Santería*, the dove was taken as a sign that Fidel had been chosen to lead the nation to its rendezvous with destiny.

From that point forward, Cubans increasingly left it up to Fidel to determine that destiny. They turned to the man, not to any particular program he outlined. Thus, it made little difference that he had promised elections but never held them. Fidel Castro was the leader. The Cuban people would follow him, whatever the program and however he wished to carry it out.

The willingness to leave everything to Fidel can also be attributed to the almost total political vacuum which existed after Batista's departure. The old political system, with its corrupt and indifferent ways, and the old economic system, with its few rich and many poor, were totally discredited. They had failed to produce an acceptable way of life, let alone national dignity. Also discredited were the institutions: the congress, the political parties, the civic and business organizations and most certainly the army.

True, compared with most other Latin American countries, Cuba was relatively well off. It had one of the highest gross national products in Latin America and the second highest standard of living, just below Argentina. But there was a tremendous disparity in who enjoyed that standard of living. There were a few who lived in incredible luxury, there was a large comfortable middle class, and then there were the 25% who lived in abject poverty.

Sugar was king, but the cane fields of the countryside provided employment for only four months of the year. The rest of the time, during the so-called dead season, many rural workers lived hand to mouth. While on a per-capita basis there were more doctors in Cuba than in any other Latin American country, there were few in the countryside, and no public health clinics. Fully 60% of the peasantry had no access to health care at all. If they got sick, they cured themselves or they died. Nor were there schools for their children. Corrupt officials in the ministry of education stole the money for teachers' salaries while what school houses there were sat empty.

In short, though Cuba was a relatively wealthy nation in terms of what it

Castro made his first

speech in Havana

following the triumph

of the Revolution.

A dove that landed

on his shoulder was

taken as a sign by

many that Castro

was the "Chosen One"

to lead Cuba, 1959.

produced, the wealth was inequitably distributed. The rural workers, who in fact produced most of the wealth, received the smallest share. Castro said he would change that. Moreover, he said he would make Cuba a fully independent nation. No longer would Cubans feel they were citizens of a second-class nation, the appendage of a more powerful neighbor. Nor were Castro's ambitions in this endeavor restricted to Cuba. As he told José "Pepin" Bosch, the head of the Bacardi Rum Company, to whom he turned as an economic adviser in early 1959, he intended to do nothing less than finish the work of the Great Liberator, Simon Bolivar. Bolivar had freed Latin America from Spanish political control. Now, Castro would free it from U.S. economic domination.

At the time, the Cuban people were content to leave the business of accomplishing all this entirely in Castro's hands. He had *carte blanche.*

And what of the United States? What position had it taken with respect to Castro's struggle against Batista?

The United States was not in any way responsible for Batista's return to power in 1952. On the contrary, the United States initially indicated its disapproval. Ambassador Willard Beaulac recommended against recognition of the Batista regime — were there any resistance to it. But there was no resistance. Consequently, the coup was accepted in Washington and relations were back to normal within a month.

Relations soon warmed beyond merely "normal," as Batista became exactly the kind of conservative military dictator favored by Washington in the early days of the Cold War and McCarthyism. As far as Washington was concerned, any Latin American leader who was vocally anti-communist and favored private enterprise was to be applauded, no matter what unfortunate practices he might be guilty of otherwise. Two Republican political-appointee ambassadors, Arthur Gardner (1954–57) and Earl E.T. Smith (1957–59) heaped praise on Batista as a bulwark against communism. In fact, Ambassador Gardner was so lavish in his words of support, even Batista found it just a bit embarrassing. "I'm glad Ambassador Gardner approves of my government," he commented to a friend. "I just wish he wouldn't talk about it so loudly." To show its full support for Batista, the United States provided military and economic assistance to Cuba.

The rebellion against Batista placed Washington in a dilemma. On the one hand, U.S. officials were suspicious of Castro, who inevitably was seen as having communist sympathies. On the other, this was clearly a civil war, and thus one in which it behooved the United States to remain neutral. Further, the Reciprocal Defense Agreement, under which U.S. arms were provided to Batista's forces, specifically stated that the aid could not be used in such a conflict. In other words, U.S. arms were not to be used against the Cuban people. Yet, by mid-1957, it was clear that Batista was so using them. To remedy the situation, Washington declared an arms embargo, but the U.S. Military Assistance Group was left in Havana to train Batista's army. Thus, in May of 1958, when the annual levy of recruits finished training and marched off to the Oriente province to participate in the summer offensive against Castro, all the officers of the U.S. military mission were on the reviewing stand to receive their salutes. Who wouldn't have questioned the neutrality of the U.S.? Fidel Castro came to his own conclusion: if the United States trained Batista's troops to fight against him, then obviously it was not neutral.

CASTRO WITH SYMBOLIC DOVES.
JANUARY 8, 1959.

Even in November of 1958, when it was clear to almost everyone on the island that Batista was finished and Castro would soon be in power, U.S. Ambassador Smith still expressed confidence that a solution would emerge from the elections which Batista had called for that month. "Batista," Smith said, "has promised fair and honest elections. I believe him."

But Smith's confidence was misplaced. The elections were transparently rigged, and Batista's hand-picked candidates naturally won. Even then, Smith continued to insist that a solution could be worked out with Batista on the island. Washington, however, finally saw the writing on the wall. In December, it sent an emissary to urge Batista to resign and get out of the country so the transition would be as bloodless as possible. With or without an emissary from the United States, Batista had little choice in the matter. He had lost.

Castro made no effort to hide the fact that one of his major goals was to end Cuba's dependency on the United States. One of his first acts was to order the U.S. Military Assistance Group out of the country. "If Batista's army was an example of how well they train troops," he pointed out, "then we can't afford to have them around our new armed forces."

Nonetheless, Castro insisted that he wanted good relations with the United

States, so long as relations were on the basis of mutual respect rather than the old one of patron to client. In April of 1959, he paid a visit to his northern neighbor to stress that point and to call for U.S. investments.

It is often forgotten that for the first six months after Castro's victory, relations between the two countries were reasonably good. The first revolutionary government consisted mostly of moderates. For example, Roberto Agramonte, who was the *Ortodoxo* candidate for the presidency in the cancelled elections of 1952, was the first foreign minister. Rúfo López Fresquét, an economist well known to U.S. businessmen, was the first minister of treasury. American companies, while grousing mildly about some aspects of the first tax reform law, applauded others and in any event continued normal operations.

As the year wore on, however, U.S.-Cuban relations came under increasing strain as Cuba swung further to the left and began to put out feelers to the Soviet Union. By mid-1960, Castro was nationalizing U.S. companies. The United States imposed a partial trade embargo in retaliation. The Soviet Union offered to buy the sugar the United States would not, and in that same year began supplying Cuba with military equipment. Finally on January 3, 1961, after Castro ordered the expulsion of all eleven U.S. diplomats from the embassy in Havana, the United States broke diplomatic relations. A little over three months later, on the eve of the Bay of Pigs invasion, Castro for the first time declared the Cuban Revolution to be socialist, and, shortly thereafter, he announced that he was a Marxist-Leninist. His evolution was near completion.

There were those who said no evolution had taken place, that Castro had been a communist all along. There is, however, no credible evidence to support this view. Despite strenuous efforts in 1957 and 1958, as it reported to the U.S. Congress, the CIA could find no links between Castro and either the Soviets or the Cuban communists. Quite the contrary, in 1953 the Cuban Communist party (called the Popular Socialist Party, PSP) had denounced Castro's attack on the Moncada barracks as a "petty bourgeois attempted putsch carried out by irresponsible elements aligned with gangsterism."

This statement became a classical bit of revisionist history. One of its authors, Fabio Grobart, the old war horse of the Communist party, years later wrote again about the Moncada attack. He then described Castro and his followers as having at the time of the attack absorbed Marxism and for all practical purposes as being Marxist-Leninists, a far cry from calling them irresponsible putschists.

Grobart's revisionism aside, the fact was that the PSP only offered support to Castro's revolution at the eleventh hour, after it was absolutely clear that he would win. And it was only well after his victory that the PSP accepted Castro as "one of the boys." For its part, Moscow provided no support whatsoever. Even after Castro won, more than a year would pass before Moscow and Havana signed their first trade agreement, and only after another three months would they get around to establishing diplomatic relations.

Sergó Mikoyán, now the editor of the Soviet publication *Latinskaya Amerika*, accompanied his father, Anastas Mikoyán, the Soviet vice-premier, on his first visit to Cuba in February of 1960. This visit and the resulting trade agreement between the two countries marked the beginning of their new relationship. Looking back on the visit, Sergó Mikoyán remembers, "Castro made no pretense of being a Marxist-

In New York, Cuban Americans celebrate the fall of Batista, January 1, 1959.

Leninist. He was a progressive Third World leader. He wanted to reduce his dependence on the United States, yes, but no one who knows anything about Marxist-Leninist doctrine and who spent an hour with Fidel at that point could have thought that he was a communist!"

Nevertheless, after declaring himself to be a Marxist-Leninist, Castro suggested that he had been one all along. He simply had not said so because the Cuban people were not ready for it. But if this were true, why would Castro choose to reject and deride communism up to the time he declared himself to be a Communist? Why in an early 1958 interview would he have belittled the Cuban Communists as having "never opposed Batista, for whom they seem to feel a close kinship"? And why in an interview the next year would he have insisted that Cuba rejected all forms of dictatorship — whether a class dictatorship, as in the Soviet Union, or the dictatorship of a single tyrant, as in Batista's case?

Castro's assertions that he was all along a devout Communist are too much an after-the-fact argument, too self-serving, to be taken at face value. Clearly, he intended to end Cuba's dependency on the United States and to carry out a radical revolution in Cuba. Initially, however, he did not seem to intend that Cuba become a Marxist-Leninist state or enter into a close relationship with the Soviet Union. Castro's decision to adopt communism seems to have been based on pragmatism, not ideology. He was, after all, determined to break away from the close hold of the United States – a decision that would certainly lead to confrontation. Castro, then, turned to the Soviet Union in order to advance his goal of breaking free of the United States. Moreover, if he was, as he put it, to turn the Andes into the Sierra Maestra of Latin America, he might well need a Soviet shield against U.S. power. His move toward the Soviet Union, in short, was dictated by pragmatic policy considerations, not ideology.

The idea at first was to turn to Moscow for assistance, but in the same way many other Third-World states had done, without themselves becoming Marxist-Leninist. In Egypt, for example, Nasser had appealed to Moscow for help in building the Aswan Dam and in arming his troops even as he arrested the leadership of the Egyptian Communist party. But Castro's uniquely exposed position only ninety miles off the shores of the most powerful nation in the world convinced him he would soon be attacked. Ad hoc assistance, he reasoned, might not be enough. His only chance of forcing the Soviet Union to come to his defense, he must have calculated, was by declaring the Cuban revolution to be socialist. It was no coincidence that he did so on the very eve of the Bay of Pigs invasion. This was a transparent effort on his part to maneuver the Soviets into coming to his support if need be. In this instance, it turned out that he did not need their support. He defeated the invasion without it. But, he no doubt asked himself, what about next time? Hence, once having made the decision, he stuck with it. He became a Communist and, in time, turned Cuba into a Marxist-Leninist state.

The Cuban people, though they had no thought or wish to enter into an alliance with Moscow, simply accepted the will of the charismatic leader. If Castro felt such an alliance was what was needed, and, subsequently, if he felt Cuba should become a Marxist-Leninist state, then so be it; the great majority of Cubans went along. Those who did not fled to Miami, or ended up in prison.

~

Castro The Man

Who was this man who so changed Cuban history and, in many ways, the history of the countries around him? It has been said that the secret to understanding Fidel Castro lies in seeing him not as a "Stalinist dictator" – a description often used by the State Department – but as a traditional Galician *caudillo*, or political chieftain. "It is not ideology that drives Fidel," says a former classmate at the University of Havana, "it is his authoritarian instincts, his conviction that only he knows the true path and therefore that everyone else must follow him."

If so, he came by these authoritarian instincts naturally. Castro's father, Angel, was from Galicia, a province of Spain noted for its

~

Fidel Castro in Washington, D.C., in 1959. The Cuban revolution was well received in the United States until its move toward the Soviet Union and Marxist-Leninist doctrine.

Young lawyer Fidel

Castro (above) at his

induction into the Cuban

Bar. Castro (opposite)

at the United Nations,

1959. His foreign policy

exploits thrust Cuba into

the role of an important

Third World power.

tough, stubborn people. Though he arrived in Cuba penniless a few years before the final war of independence, Angel managed over the years to become a landowner and a prominent citizen of the district of Birán, in Oriente province. A bear of a man over six feet tall, he was renowned for his fiery temper, stubbornness of purpose and dominating ways, characteristics he obviously passed on to at least one of his sons.

Fidel Castro was the third of seven children born to Angel and Lina Rúz. Lina Rúz, Angel's second wife, had been the housemaid while Angel was still married to his first wife, Maria Luisa. When Lina became pregnant, Maria Luisa left her husband. Eventually, they were divorced and Angel married Lina in a church. But this did not occur until after their first three children, Angela, Ramon and Fidel, were born. It has been speculated that being born out of wedlock left a deep psychological scar on Castro, making him resentful of a society in which he was an outcast. This theory is probably more exaggeration than fact. Being born out of wedlock was not so unusual in the rural Cuba of that day, with its highly tolerant social mores. Furthermore, any stigma that might have been attached to him, or to Ramon and Angela, was certainly muted by the fact that their parents subsequently married, after which they had four more children: Juana, Raúl, Emma and Augustina. The family was accepted as members in good standing of the community, and their father was a relatively wealthy man who provided well for them and sent them to good schools in Santiago and Havana. As Ramon, the eldest brother, once said, "Not only were we fully recognized by our father, but we were the children of a loving relationship. We counted ourselves fortunate."

By the time Fidel was born on August 13, 1926, the Castro family plantation embraced almost 26,000 acres, though Angel leased most of the land. It was worked by the 300 families who lived on the plantation as laborers or sharecroppers. Despite his significant wealth, Angel always considered himself to be a "rich peasant," not a member of the landholding class. In fact, he identified with the poor and had a hearty disdain for the upper classes and social convention, something else he passed on to his famous son.

Fidel's father also passed along his resentment of the United States. To the end of his life, Angel Castro felt a certain loyalty to the Spanish motherland. He believed that the United States had stolen Cuba from Spain when the latter was virtually defenseless. To him, this was an act of treachery which he never forgave.

The "iron-willed

crusader" making

a speech in the

defiant style that

has long been

his trademark.

In addition to the traits inherited from his Galician father, there were a number of other things about Birán and Fidel's childhood there that helped shape his character and future political views. Reinforcing the resentment of the United States learned at his father's knee, the area around Nipe Bay, a few miles to the west of the Castro home, was dominated more than any other province in Cuba by American-owned sugar plantations and mills, the largest being the United Fruit complex at Preston. Fidel saw the area as a microcosm of Cuba's domination by American interests, which he, like his father, thought had been unfairly established. In a speech in 1968 he said, "They came with bulging pockets to a country impoverished by thirty years of war to buy the best land of this country for less than six dollars the hectare."

The Castro home was also near the spot where José Martí had been killed in 1895. All Cuban schoolboys admired Martí. The young Fidel's feelings went beyond admiration. Experiencing something of a backyard link to the fallen hero's place of martyrdom, Fidel vowed not only to pattern his life on Martí's, but to carry on his work.

Castro (above) was an

Finally, Fidel grew up with the children of peasants. He saw their simplicity, their goodness, their long-suffering tolerance. At the same time, he saw the poverty and ignorance to which they were condemned. It stirred in him a deep sense of injustice, one that had to be undone. As he wrote to a friend from prison in 1954, the only way to undo it was to completely change the system: "Nothing that could be done in the domain of…education can lead anywhere unless one reshuffles from top to bottom the economic status of the nation…because that is where the real root of the tragedy lies."

excellent baseball player

in his youth. Opposite,

he winds up at Latin

American Stadium.

Clearly, one can trace back to Fidel's childhood the two overriding characteristics of his later life. First, he was determined to change things, to lift up the dispossessed and downtrodden. And second, he sensed himself to be a champion, the leader of a

just cause, whose command in the rightful order of things must be obeyed. Those who did not obey were outside that order and therefore open to just retribution.

Fidel was also the product of a Jesuit education, first at the hands of the priests at the Dolores School in Santiago, then at the exclusive Belén School in Havana. Not always jokingly, members of other Catholic orders have suggested that this helps to explain his militancy, his unbending dedication to a cause. As one Cuban priest has said of him, "Essentially, Fidel is an iron-willed crusader, a man consumed by his mission and willing to sacrifice everything for it. He is a man perhaps more attuned to past centuries, yes, and whose cause I reject. Nonetheless, I recognize the type. He is one who in other circumstances and other times would have died with his Indian converts in the missions of Paraguay."

After graduating from Belen in 1945, Castro spent five years at the University of Havana, finishing with a law degree in 1950. Immediately thereafter, he began a law practice, and having helped found the *Ortodoxo* party in 1947, he went into politics. On the eve of Batista's seizure of power in June of 1952, Castro was running for a seat in Cuba's House of Representatives.

What of Castro's personal life? Certainly he has had little time for it since coming to power in 1959. He normally works an eighteen to twenty-hour day, usually sleeping only a few hours between four or five and nine in the morning, more often than not in the bedroom next to his office at Central Committee headquarters. His son Fidel Castro, Jr., who is one of the Soviet-trained directors of the Cuban nuclear-power program, prefers to stay in the background and is said

FIDEL CUTTING SUGAR CANE IN
ORIENTE PROVINCE. 1967

~ He was an old man who fished alone in a skiff in the Gulf Stream and he had gone eighty-four days now without taking a fish. In the first forty days a boy had been with him. But after forty days without a fish the boy's parents had told him that the old man was now definitely and finally *salao*, which is the worst form of unlucky, and the boy had gone at their orders into another boat which caught three good fish in the first week. It made the boy sad to see the old man come in each day with his skiff empty and he always went down to help him carry either the coiled lines or the gaff and harpoon and the sail that was furled around the mast. The sail was patched with flour sacks and, furled, it looked like the flag of permanent defeat. ~

FROM *THE OLD MAN AND THE SEA*
BY ERNEST HEMINGWAY

With the exception of José Martí, Hemingway

(left) is the most widely read author in Cuba.

Castro (above) with

his inner circle, Raúl

Castro (center) and

Ché Guevara (right).

to have little interest in politics. He and his father are, nevertheless, very close and Castro reportedly adores his grandchildren. At their parents wish, however, the children are never seen with him in public.

Since his divorce in 1954, there have been other women in Fidel's life. The most important by far was Celia Sanchez Manduley, who joined him in the mountains and was his confidante, friend, mistress, secretary and aide. Although by 1977, their relationship was probably platonic, she continued to be the one person in the world closest to him, probably the only one he fully trusted. In 1979, Marta Solís, a Mexican newspaper reporter who knew them both well, described their relationship in the following terms, "Celia Sanchez is all things to Fidel. She is his compass, his conscience, and always his solace. No one has the influence with him that she does. No one will ever mean more to him than she does."

Even most anti-Castro Cubans acknowledge that Celia Sanchez's influence over Fidel was generally humane and for the best. It was because of her that many opponents were spared and that many Catholic families were able to depart safely from Cuba even during the height of the church-state clash in the early 1960s. A woman of immense warmth and love for the Cuban people, she was, in turn, revered by them. Her death in January 1980 was cause for national mourning. Castro was disconsolate. Indeed, a number of the questionable decisions he made at that time may have resulted from the fact that he had lost "his compass," as Marta Solís might have put it. For example, the decision to allow the Mariel Exodus, which proved deeply embarrassing to the Cuban government, was made not long

CHÉ AND FIDEL FISHING
IN BARLOVENTO. 1960.

after her death. It was some time before Fidel regained his composure.

Important though she was, Celia Sanchez was not the only woman to share a part of Castro's life. Another was Marita Lorenz, the beautiful 17-year-old daughter of a German sea captain whose ship sailed into Havana in February of 1959. Quite by chance, Castro went aboard. He and Marita met and apparently the attraction was instant. When the ship sailed, Marita remained behind sharing Castro's suite at the Havana Hilton (soon to be nationalized and renamed the *Havana Libré*). She was his companion for almost a year, then went to Miami. For a time she worked with the CIA, which assigned her to live with the deposed Venezuelan dictator Marcos Perez Jimenez, apparently to keep him under surveillance. Subsequently, she became disillusioned with the agency's methods and left its employment.

Celia Sanchez Manduley (above) was Castro's closest confidante until her death in 1980. Marita Lorenz (below) the daughter of a German sea captain, was Castro's companion for almost a year before working briefly for the CIA.

Despite her brief CIA connection, Castro permitted Lorenz to return to Cuba for a visit in 1980 and they remain on good terms today.

Marita Lorenz was by no means the only "other woman." There have been many. An article in the Moscow newspaper *Komsomolskaya Pravda* in November of 1990 alleged that Castro has had a secret wife and many mistresses, ideas that came as no surprise to most Cubans. Indeed, Cuban officials have long acknowledged discreetly that *El Comandante* has fathered children around the island. Some Cubans call him *"El Caballo"* (the Horse) because of the incident with the dove, when supposedly he was mounted by the gods, an earthier explanation refers to his sexual prowess.

Be that as it may, especially since the death of Celia Sanchez in 1980, the impression is that Castro is a lonely, isolated man. Celia and Ché Guevara and others close to him, who told him when they thought he was making a mistake, are gone. Those who remain, with the exception of his brother Raúl, dare not disagree. One does not question a living legend unless one has a special relationship with him. Raúl, the one person who has such a relationship, is not inclined to disagree. He is the younger brother trailing in the older's wake. As a Western European diplomat in Havana has put it, "The Cuban ship of state sails on, with only one man at the helm, and the crew fearful of warning him should he steer toward the rocks. Were I a passenger, I would be most concerned."

Such is the classic dilemma of the authoritarian ruler.

The Paradox of Revolution

With the collapse of communism in Eastern Europe during 1989, pundits in the United States have speculated that Cuba will inevitably be the next to go. Whether or not the communist system in Cuba eventually collapses, the analogy with Eastern Europe is misplaced. Communism was imposed on the Eastern bloc countries at the point of a Soviet bayonet. By and large, the communist leaders were also imposed. None ever had a shred of popularity; rather, they remained in power because of the looming shadow of the Soviet Union. The most certain consequences, should popular forces try to unseat them, were stamped in blood on the streets of Budapest, Hungary, in 1956 and Prague,

~

The beauty of an island sunset is interrupted by smokestacks along Havana Harbor. Antiquated factories and power plants have limited pollution controls and are in dire need of modernization.

Czechoslovakia, in 1968. But once Mikhail Gorbachev said Moscow would no longer maintain the communist governments of Eastern Europe in power by force, their demise was inevitable, though the rapidity with which the end came surprised almost everyone.

The situation in Cuba has been very different. Castro came to power at the head of his own tremendously popular nationalist revolution. The ultimate charismatic leader, he was the greatest national hero since José Martí. The Cuban people placed their confidence in him and supported — even if with misgivings — his decision to transform Cuba into a communist state. True, his popular support has eroded over the years as economic problems have mounted. The Cuban people have simply grown tired of sacrificing — tired of working hard for limited rewards, tired of food rationing, tired of waiting for the better life that has failed to materialize.

It is no longer clear that Castro would win an election — should he ever choose to hold one, which isn't likely. But, even with all the problems he faces, Castro has at least until now retained more popular support than the Eastern European leaders ever dreamed of having.

Although after thirty years the Cuban Revolution has not managed to produce the promised utopia, there have been benefits. Few Czechs would have said they were better off under communism than under their own democratic government before 1938. However, at least until their recent difficulties, many Cubans were better off under Castro than under previous governments. Though Castro has not allowed a free press or free elections, those things were circumscribed under Batista as well. Under the Revolution, there has been no unemployment, homelessness, or malnourishment. In Cuba after 1959, one did not see beggars and the sick and lame without treatment. Nor did one see the masses of people living in abject poverty and misery that fill the slums surrounding almost every other Latin American capital. Cubans may have to stand in long lines to get rations, and their diet may be monotonous, but no one goes hungry.

The Cuban Revolution virtually wiped out illiteracy and provides education through the postgraduate level to anyone who can pass the tests. No more are the sons and daughters of peasants trapped in ignorance. They have schools; they can go to the University; and, if they have the talent, they can become doctors, engineers, computer technicians, or most anything else.

Since the Revolution, Cubans have also had excellent and virtually free medical care. Clinics were built in the countryside so that even the poorest and most isolated peasant families have a doctor nearby. Nor are advances restricted to the area of general practice. Great strides have also been made in specialized medicine. So much so that many Latin Americans now come to Cuba for the treatment of orthopedic problems, burns, nerve and motor disfunctions and various other specialized disorders. As a gesture of their solidarity with the Russian people and to emphasize how advanced their medicine is, the Cubans have recently been treating children affected by, injured in or suffering from the after effects of the Chernobyl accident.

Cuba has also sent thousands of doctors — often at no cost to the host governments — to countries in Africa, the Middle East and the Caribbean Basin. Moreover, Cuba's infant mortality rate is the lowest in the Third World. Indeed, it is lower than the rate in many U.S. cities.

The Cuban Revolution has assured its citizens of the basic material needs. Although without frills, Cubans nonetheless tend to be better fed, better housed and generally better cared for than the masses of citizens in neighboring countries such as Honduras, El Salvador, Guatemala and Mexico, to say nothing of Haiti.

Cubans, however, do not compare their way of life with that of the average Honduran or Guatemalan. Rather, they compare it with that of their brothers, sisters or cousins in Miami. Inevitably theirs is found wanting. Further, while the basic needs have been guaranteed until this point, given the chaos in the Soviet Union and the breakdown in Soviet deliveries of wheat, petroleum and other necessities, no one knows how long that will remain the case.

If the economic picture has been mixed, so has the political situation. Castro's Revolution ended Cuba's former dependence of the United States and gave the Cuban people a strong sense of national identity and pride. One of Cuba's leading poets, Pablo Armando Fernandez, has described that change in terms of his personal feelings:

"When I lived in New York back in the 1950s, I used to tell people I was an Argentine. Cuba after all, was only a banana republic. A country with corrupt presidents where Americans went to get drunk. But then came the Cuban Revolution. Since then,

Lines at a liquor store in Havana. The revolution requires patience, but the Cuban people have grown tired of sacrificing and tired of waiting for the better life that has failed to fully materialize.

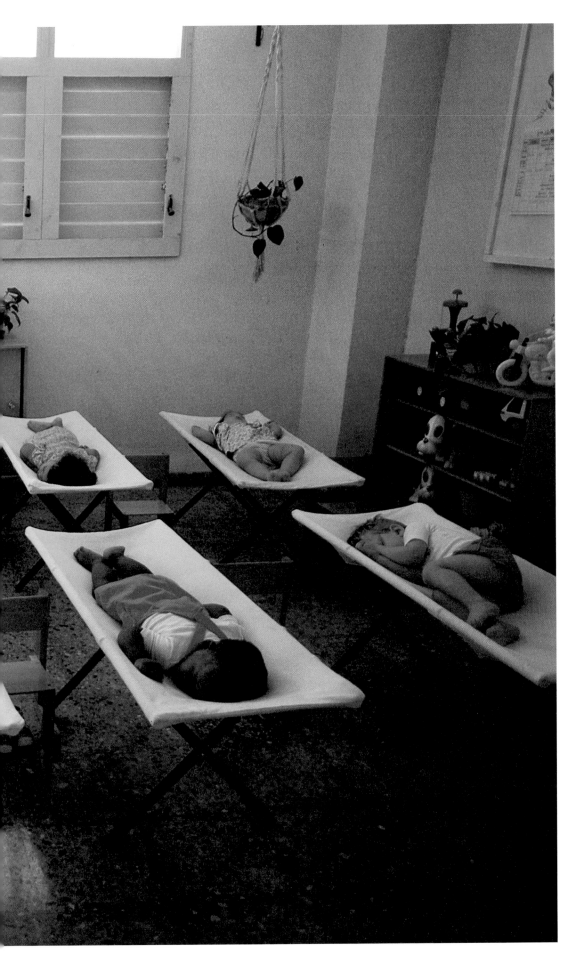

The I Dream of Ché Daycare Center *in Havana. From birth, the state provides for the basic needs of the individual. That has been the promise of Castro's revolution. In return, it demands unswerving obedience.*

whether you agree with Castro or not, he has projected Cuba onto the world stage in a way we Cubans can be proud of. Cuban troops turned back the South Africans and saved Angola. Cuba became one of the principal forces in the Non-Aligned Movement."

While the Revolution inspired pride where before there had been degradation, on the other side of the coin, it had no tolerance for those who disagreed. Anyone who went along with Castro and his decision to construct a Marxist-Leninist system had a place in the pattern of things. Those who did not agree and said so were likely to end up behind bars or shot, unless they took the course followed by almost one million Cubans and fled to the United States.

Social upheavals of the magnitude of the Cuban Revolution, in which a whole ruling class and system are displaced, inevitably result in personal tragedies and suffering. There were massive arrests in the early 1960s, especially after the Bay of Pigs debacle. Pro-Castro Cubans argue they had no choice but to put counter-revolutionary elements behind bars. After all, they contend, Cuba was virtually at war with the United States, and the CIA had agents all over the island dedicated to the overthrow of the new regime. They also point out that a good percentage of American colonists moved to Canada after the American Revolution rather than live under the new political system that became the United States. Hence, it should not be surprising that many Cubans, especially the large landholders and the wealthy, opted to take exile in Miami.

While there is truth in this argument, it does not diminish the tragedy of the human suffering involved. But there is another dimension to the repression that took place. It is said that revolutions devour their children. If so, the Cuban Revolution was certainly no exception. Members of the former government and the economic elite were not the only ones to end up behind bars. Many who fought with Castro against Batista suffered the same fate. One either followed Castro totally, or one was likely to be considered an enemy. For example, Major Hubér Matos fought in the Sierra Maestra and in October of 1959 was the military commander of the Camaguey province. Seeing that Castro was moving to the left and allowing the old-line Communists to play an ever greater role in the government, Matos wrote Castro a letter expressing his disagreement and offering to resign quietly. A day later, Matos was brought to Havana in chains and sentenced to twenty years in prison. He was released in 1979 and now lives in the United States.

Don Soldini, the young New Yorker, was one of the lucky ones. Though arrested in 1959 when he protested what he saw as the unfair imprisonment of two Americans, Soldini was released on Fidel Castro's orders. He and Castro even had dinner together in the Havana Hilton the night before Soldini left Cuba for good. "I knew it was time to go," Soldini says now. "Things were not going as we'd hoped. I and others like me had hoped for a fully democratic government. Castro was clearly beginning to get other ideas."

The colorful American paratrooper William Morgan

Empty shelves in what was a F.W. Woolworth's before the revolution. In contemporary Cuba, shopping is less a matter of preference or need than availability.

was given the job of running a frog farm after the fighting was over. Later, however, he was arrested and shot for counterrevolutionary activities. His former commander in the Second Front Escambray, Eloy Gutierrez Menoyo, was arrested, released, left Cuba, then returned to head a guerrilla group, was captured again and given a long prison sentence. Released in 1987, he now lives in Spain.

One could add hundreds of other names to the list, men and women who fought to get rid of Batista and to build a better Cuba. Their only sin was that their conception of what would constitute a better Cuba did not coincide with Fidel's.

By the mid 1960s, there were as many as 60,000 political prisoners in Cuba's jails — most held under truly appalling conditions. Men were worked to death, beaten, even bayoneted by the guards. Cuban officials may deny that such conditions existed, but there are too many thousands of released prisoners who witnessed them for such denials to be credible.

Fortunately, conditions began to improve in the mid-1970s. A penal reform program closed most of the old prisons, some dating to colonial days, and new, modern facilities were built. Under the reform program, many prisoners were released and conditions improved for those who remained. By 1979, there were only an estimated 5,000 political prisoners behind bars, most of whom were freed as the result of negotiations with the Carter Administration.

In addition to jailing those who disagreed with him, Castro quickly imposed tight controls on Cuban society. Under Batista, a newspaper editor who criticized the regime might be beaten up by the dictator's thugs, but at least there were independent newspapers which, if editors had the courage, could provide a version of events other than the government's. Under Castro, all independent newspapers were closed. Since 1965, only those controlled by the Communist party or the government have been in operation.

It is fair to say that under Castro, Cubans have lost even the tenuous civil and political liberties they had under the old regime. Cuba is a one-party state. The people do not elect their national leaders, nor can they freely express themselves. Woe to anyone who gets on a soap box in downtown Havana and questions the wisdom of the Castro government.

Few would do so. Over the years, the Cuban people have learned what is permissible and what is not. Most choose to live within the parameters of what is. Thus, the massive arrests and draconian measures of the 1960s are no longer necessary. Most of the hard-core opponents, the so-called class enemies, long ago fled to Miami. Also, the rules governing freedom of expression are now so well understood by all involved that subtle measures more than suffice.

Be that as it may, the fact remains that Cuba has been a police state of sorts since the early 1960s. Castro kept his promises to better the lot of the peasants and the urban poor, but he quickly forgot the promise to restore the freedoms guaranteed in the Constitution of 1940. As one Cuban put it, "We traded our dreams of a democratic system for a guaranteed bowl of socialist soup."

The **Villa Vento** *is one of the many state-run love hotels or* **posadas**. *Only couples are admitted. Most costumers are married — sometimes to each other. The* **posadas** *are open 24 hours a day, 365 days a year.*

Embracing The Bear

The Cuban-Soviet alliance was a marriage of convenience, with Castro the eager bride and the Soviet Union the suspicious, initially reluctant groom. Though U.S. Ambassador Earl E.T. Smith claimed Castro had always been a communist, the Soviets did not know him as such and wondered if they could really trust him. It was one thing to buy sugar from him and give some aid, but the Soviets did not want to commit themselves beyond that. During 1959 and into 1960, Khrushchev was going all out to reach an accommodation with the United States. Therefore, he did not want to meddle too brazenly in the U.S. backyard if the result would torpedo his hopes for detente. But in early May of 1960, an American U-2

Nikita Khrushchev and Fidel Castro meet for the first time at the Hotel Theresa in Harlem in the Fall of 1960.

reconnaissance aircraft piloted by Gary Powers was shot down over the Soviet Union. As a consequence, the Paris Summit held a few days later between Eisenhower and Khrushchev ended in a stalemate.

With hopes for detente thus consigned to the shelf, some of Khrushchev's caution regarding Cuba disappeared. Aid commitments increased, and the Communist bloc countries began to supply Cuba with weaponry. However, Moscow continued to refuse an all-out embrace. Although from April of 1961 forward Castro insisted that the Cuban Revolution was socialist, to recognize Cuba as a socialist state — the ideological sister of the Soviet Union — would have imposed greater risks and commitments than the Soviets were willing to accept at the time. They were under no obligation to come to the defense of a progressive, national-liberation state like Cuba. Such a doctrinal obligation did exist, however, with respect to sister socialist states. Thus, it was not until May of 1962, after Khrushchev had already decided to place missiles in Cuba, that Moscow finally acknowledged Cuba as a socialist state. By then it served Soviet interests to do so, for if the missiles were to be emplaced, it was better that they were on the soil of a socialist country.

Not surprisingly, from mid-1962 forward, Soviet economic and military assistance flowed generously. The Soviets recognized the advantages of Cuba as a strategic base and also as a potential showcase of what a socialist economy could achieve. They hoped Cuba might be portrayed as the model of a socialist tomorrow in the Western Hemisphere. If Cuba showed strong growth and provided improved services for its people, other Latin American states might decide to follow its example. Cuba never became that model. Though it provided improved services, its economic performance was never as impressive as either the Soviets or the Cubans had hoped. Nonetheless, for a time the fact that its people had health care and enough to eat made Cuba look good when compared to some of its neighbors.

If Moscow saw Cuba as an important toehold in Latin America, essentially what Castro hoped to get out of the bargain was protection from the United States. He wanted a shield against U.S. power behind which he could pursue his own goals in Latin America, principally, his desire to turn the Andes into the Sierra Maestra of Latin America. Beyond protection, he also wanted and needed Soviet economic support. Pre-revolutionary Cuba had been heavily dependent on the United States. More that 60% of its trade was with the U.S., and virtually all the machinery on the island, from cars and refrigerators to industrial plants, originated there. With its link to the United States cut by the trade embargo Washington began to impose in mid-1960, Cuba had to look elsewhere for new markets and sources of supply. Albeit slowly and reluctantly, Moscow responded, and by mid-1962, the Soviets had supplanted the United States in providing both. Eventually, most American-made machinery was phased out and replaced by equipment manufactured in the Soviet Union and Eastern Europe. By the mid-sixties, more than half of Cuba's trade was with the Soviet Union.

There was one small problem that had to be resolved before Cuba could *truly* be a Marxist-Leninist state. A sacrosanct tenet of Communist doctrine at that time was that socialist states be ruled by a vanguard Communist party. As of 1962, Cuba's was not; rather, Castro's 26th of July Movement was the ruling party. A number of old-line communists held high positions in the government, but the Party

itself remained to one side, undermining Cuba's definition as a socialist state.

Castro set about to remedy the situation by simply forming a new Cuban Communist Party (CCP) composed of the old party, his own 26th of July Movement, the Revolutionary Directorate (DR) and a few splinter groups. It was patterned after the Communist Party of the Soviet Union (CPSU), with a Central Committee and a Politburo, the latter being the most powerful decision-making body on the island. He soon reorganized the Cuban state along Soviet lines, with a Council of Ministers and a system of popular assemblies roughly equivalent to the System of Soviets (or councils) in the USSR. Cuba's assemblies began at the municipal level and culminated in the National Assembly of People's Power, Cuba's answer to the Supreme Soviet. The National Assembly had little real power, its principal function being to rubber stamp the decisions already made by the Politburo of the CCP.

Though delegates to the municipal councils were chosen through direct elections, that was as far as direct elections went. The members of the municipal councils themselves decided who would represent them in the provincial assemblies and in the National Assembly.

All the political machinery of government aside, the fact was that Fidel, as first secretary of the Politburo, president of the Council of State of the National Assembly, and president of the Council of Ministers, made all the key decisions. No reorganization changed that. Whatever he was called, Fidel was the *caudillo* or chief.

Relations between the two new partners were still far from harmonious. Behind the shield provided by the Soviets, Castro expected to pursue his objectives in Latin America in his own way. He wanted to see the other governments of the

A portrait of Lenin hangs over the doorway of a state commissary that distributes ration cards. Cuba's unique brand of communism mixes the basic principles of Marxism with a distinctive Latin verve.

hemisphere replaced by revolutionary regimes, and he was convinced that this could be accomplished only through armed struggle. "The duty of all true revolutionaries," he said during those years, "is to take rifle in hand and begin the revolution."

The Soviets did not agree. They did not believe armed revolution could succeed in the other countries; rather, they feared it would provoke a U.S. reaction and perhaps bring about the destruction of the orthodox communist parties the Soviets had nurtured so carefully through the years. Thus, those parties were to follow peaceful, low-key tactics, not armed struggle. When Castro became an ally, the Soviets expected him to accept the same tactics and work through Moscow's orthodox Communist parties, not through the guerilla groups that, inspired by the Cuban example, had sprung up all over the hemisphere.

Castro would have none of it. The international communist movement, he said, was not the Roman Catholic Church. Moscow was not Rome, and there was no pope. Each party had to interpret Marxism-Leninism for itself and adapt it to local conditions. Moreover, he pointed out, no one could tell him how to make a revolution.

Perhaps nothing more sharply magnifies the gap between Russians and Cubans than the fact that Russians do not play baseball — the national passion of Cuba.

He had already made one, and had done it on his own without any help or advice from Moscow.

To say the least, Cuban-Soviet relations were not helped by the outcome of the missile crisis in October, 1962. Fully understanding the risks and prepared to accept them, Castro agreed to the emplacement of the Soviet missiles. Cuba and the Soviet Union, he thought, would now stand shoulder to shoulder against any U.S. demand that the missiles be withdrawn. Wrong. He awoke one morning to hear on the radio that Khrushchev had reached an agreement with Kennedy to remove the missiles. He had not even been advised that such a deal was in the works. That the price was a pledge from Kennedy not to invade Cuba was beside the point. Castro was furious that the two superpowers had struck a deal behind his back. Though Khrushchev had agreed that the United Nations could supervise the dismantling of the missiles, Castro refused to allow it. After all, it was his country. The Soviets finessed Castro's refusal by taking the missiles out as uncovered deck cargo, so that American planes could count them and verify their withdrawal. But they could not finesse Castro's anger. In November, when Soviet Vice-Premier Anastas Mikoyan arrived on a feather-smoothing mission, Castro would not even receive him. Mikoyan was kept waiting for weeks, until finally, in January of 1963, he begged an audience so that he could return home for the funeral of his wife.

Eventually, Castro's fury cooled to the point that he could again transact normal business with the Soviets. Relations remained poor for many years, however, with the dispute over tactics continuing through most of the sixties.

Ché Guevara, who had taken to scathing criticism of Moscow for what he saw as its craven refusal to help guerrilla movements and confront imperialism on a broad front, left Cuba in 1965 under mysterious circumstances. He went to the Congo to organize guerrilla warfare, then to Bolivia in 1967, where he was defeated and killed.❊ There have been rumors and speculation that the Soviets forced Castro to get rid of Guevara, whom they considered entirely too outspoken, though there has never been any hard evidence of this. Whether or not the rumors were true, it is clear at least that the Soviets were delighted to see Guevara go.

Guevara's defeat marked a new turning point, for it revealed dramatically the failure of Castro's guerrilla-warfare tactics, at least in Latin America. Though Castro aided them with arms as well as inspiration and advice, rural guerrilla movements everywhere were on the defensive by the latter part of the decade. A number had been defeated outright.

Doubtless the Soviets, whose fears had been justified, increased pressure on Castro to accept their less confrontational approach in Latin America. By the end of the decade, with his own tactics a failure and under constant Soviet goading, Castro began to move away from support for armed struggle. He would hold to it in a few countries where the conditions for revolution seemed especially propitious, such as Nicaragua and El Salvador. Otherwise, he began to reach out to establish diplomatic relations with the same governments he once vowed to overthrow.

With their principal dispute resolved, relations between Havana and Moscow improved markedly. Though they continued to have disagreements, over the years the Cubans and Soviets learned to deal quietly with one another. Indeed, Cuba became Moscow's most loyal supporter. It backed Soviet positions around the world and in Africa played a role that was not only useful to its superpower ally, but, also won the admiration of the Soviet military.

Even during the warmest moments of their relationship, however, there was never much rapport or human understanding between them. Cubans were genuinely grateful for Soviet assistance, without which they could not have survived U.S. economic and military efforts against them. But they never warmed to the Russians as people. Cubans are fun-loving and relaxed; they have an irreverent sense of humor. Nothing is more to their liking than poking fun at arrogance and pomposity. The perennial underdog, they are suspicious of big, powerful countries, including the Soviet Union. Inevitably, the rather somber, even stodgy, Russians with their superpower complexes became the butt of an impressive array of Cuban jokes. For example, Russians were called "bowling pins" because, as the Cubans put it, "They are fat and haven't the sense to get out of the way of the ball; they just stand there stolidly, waiting to get hit."

The Soviets had a certain admiration for Cuba's grit, but tended to see the

---

❊Guevara's band was tracked down by Bolivian forces aided by American Green Berets and CIA advisers. After a fierce battle, Guevara was captured. Fearing that as a prisoner he would become a rallying symbol to insurgents, the Bolivians executed him and buried him in an unmarked grave after amputating and preserving both his hands as proof of his death.

Cubans themselves as disorganized and prone to put things off until *mañana*. A Soviet complaint (not unfamiliar in the United States with respect to its own aid recipients) was that they were throwing their aid money down a rat hole. "The problem here is not lack of funds, but the failure of the Cubans to utilize those funds more effectively," a Soviet technician complained in 1982.

Cubans, on the other hand, often complained that the Soviets were too inflexible, that they could not adapt their methods and technology to a tropical climate.

But perhaps nothing more sharply magnifies the gap between Russians and Cubans than the fact that the Russians do not play baseball, which is a national passion with the Cubans. By the same token, Cubans do not play soccer or hockey, national passions with the Soviets. The importance of baseball in Cuba can hardly be exaggerated. Even today, a baseball game is virtually a ritual, as anyone who has seen a game in Havana's huge *America Latina* stadium can fully appreciate. The crowds cheer wildly for each key play and dance the mambo or the lambada in the aisles to the throb of bongo drums. Americans might understand and eventually feel a part of the ritual. Russians find that impossible.

This is not to say that the Cuban-Soviet alliance has not been an effective one. It has been. However, that political-military alliance is never likely to deepen into a profound friendship. The two countries are simply too different for that.

Still, the political-military alliance has created certain bonds between the two nations. Many Soviet military men stationed for years in Cuba, or perhaps even who fought alongside the Cubans in Ethiopia or Angola, speak with fond admiration of their Cuban comrades in arms. Here there is obviously a good deal of camaraderie, for there is also a continuing mutual interest. But Cuba is of declining strategic importance to the Soviet Union. No Soviet bombers fly out of Cuban airfields, and there are no Soviet submarine bases in Cuba. Indeed, no Soviet nuclear-missile submarine has even been in a Cuban port since 1974. In keeping with the terms of the Kennedy-Khrushchev understanding, there have been no nuclear weapons of any kind in Cuba since 1962. With the end of the Cold War, it is not likely that any would ever be returned there.

The Soviets do have one asset in Cuba that is still important to them, however, the huge electronic surveillance facility at Lourdes, right outside of Havana. From the facility, the Soviets can monitor most telephonic and radio communications on the U.S. eastern seaboard. As the United States and the Soviet Union move toward sweeping agreements on the reduction of nuclear weapons, Lourdes becomes a key means for the Soviets to verify U.S. compliance. One Soviet diplomat in Washington said in 1990, "The time may come when we will not need the Lourdes facility, but for now it is more important to us than ever."

There are other kinds of bonds between the two peoples, such as the Cubans' care of the "Chernobyl children." Since 1987, thousands of these small victims from the Chernobyl nuclear disaster have been brought to *Ciudad de los Pioneros* (Pioneer City), a retreat where school-aged Cuban children spend two weeks of the year. The Soviet children receive free medical treatment and time in the sun. Dr. Carlos Dotres Martinez, the director of the project, explains that the program is in keeping with Cuba's commitment to international humanitarian aid:

> We have thousands of doctors in the developing countries around
> the world — often in places where there would be no doctors or

any form of health care were it not for us. If we can help these
unfortunate children, of course we should do so. It is our duty as
internationalists, and it is also a means of showing our appreciation
for the aid given us in the past by the Soviet people.

Dr. Dotres might have added that it is an effort on Cuba's part that continues
despite a new challenge to Cuban-Soviet relations. This rift began to appear in
1989, as communist governments in Eastern Europe collapsed and the Soviet
Union moved toward a more democratic political system and a market economy.
With these developments, Cuba faces a very different world, and certainly drastic
changes can be expected in the Cuban-Soviet relationship.

One of the many Chernobyl children treated in Cuban hospitals. The level of health care in Cuba is unusually high for a Third World country and surpasses that of some industrialized nations.

AN UNCLE SAM TARGET AT A HAVANA ARCADE

In the Shadow of The Giant

For more than thirty years, Cuba has been one of the most emotional issues in American foreign policy. Cuba seems to have the same effect on American administrations that the full moon used to have on werewolves.*

Not that the disagreements and conflicts of interests between the United States and Cuba are as imaginary as the hair-sprouting force of the moon. On the contrary, they are all too real. But the same American leaders who speak quite rationally of dealings with other countries with which we have disagreements — such as the Soviet Union, the Peoples Republic of China, Syria, South Africa and even Vietnam — angrily reject that possibility with respect to Cuba.

For more than thirty years, Castro has used David and Goliath imagery to portray the relationship between Cuba and the United States.

❋Wayne Smith as quoted in the New York Times.

In part, this is probably because of history. Americans were accustomed to thinking of Cuba virtually as an American protectorate, which received its independence as the result of U.S. generosity. It was a place where Americans went on the weekends to have a good time. In short, it was ours. Cuba's decision to break away and, worse, to move into an association with our sworn enemy, the Soviet Union, violated what Americans saw as the rightful pattern of things. If Cubans were not grateful to the United States, it must be because they were a pack of ingrates.

There was also Fidel Castro's defiant style. The image most American leaders have had of him is of a bearded pip-squeak (he may be big, but his country is not) who has jeered at us, blown cigar smoke in our faces and kicked us in the shins for over thirty years. To say Castro was never popular in Washington is an understatement.

Hostility was not a one-way street, however. Breaking away from the United States was, after all, Castro's overriding objective. Still, he at first insisted he wanted good relations with Washington, as long as it was based on equality rather than the old patron-client status. And, despite suspicions about Castro, Washington did at least make an early effort to establish a good working relationship with his government. The United States extended recognition quickly and sent a highly competent career ambassador, Philip W. Bonsal, with instructions to hold out the hand of friendship. Finally, during Castro's April, 1959, visit to Washington, U.S. officials even suggested the possibility of economic assistance, should Castro wish to discuss it. He did not. Though he did not publicly reject the offer, the fact was that U.S. economic assistance would have been inconsistent with his efforts to break free of any dependency on the United States. Still, the offer was made, an indication of Washington's initial hopes of reaching an accommodation with Castro.

While Washington and Castro originally said they wanted good relations, the dynamics of the situation carried them almost inexorably toward confrontation. Castro's campaign to assert Cuba's full independence included a good deal of anti-American rhetoric. It also included the nationalization of U.S. properties and the adoption in international forums of positions that often clashed with those of the United States.

The United States reacted negatively to all this. To some extent, it could hardly do otherwise. Governments do have an obligation to defend the interests of their citizens abroad. A diplomatic note protesting the nationalization of properties without adequate compensation was the least the U.S. embassy in Havana could do in that regard. Castro, however, regarded each American protest note and expression of concern as confirmation of his worst suspicions of Washington's aggressive intentions. "Eventually," he told an advisor, "the yankees will try to destroy us; we must be prepared for the worst."

His response was to voice even more defiance and to move closer to the Soviets, a reaction which further alarmed Washington. Relations had so deteriorated by March of 1960 that President Eisenhower authorized the CIA to initiate actions against Cuba — authorization that eventually led to the organization of the Cuban-exile invasion force for the Bay of Pigs operation. The United States and Cuba came to a formal break in diplomatic relations on January 3, 1961. However, by then it was a meaningless gesture, for all trade relations had already been severed,

Planes burn at a Cuban airfield on April 14, 1961. The Bay of Pigs fiasco began with the bombing of four Cuban airfields by U.S. B-26s disguised by the CIA with Cuban Airforce markings.

MISSILE ERECTOR

CABLE

MISSILE SHELTER TENT

TRACKED PRIME MOVERS

FUEL TANK TRAILERS

OXIDIZER TANK TRAILERS

A low altitude reconnaissance photograph taken October 23, 1962 reveals the build-up of Soviet nuclear missiles in San Cristobal, Cuba.

all U.S. properties on the island had been nationalized, Cuban assets in the United States had been frozen and most members of the large American colony in Cuba had long since departed.

Washington was now determined to get rid of Castro and thought there was an easy way to do so. In 1954, the CIA had overthrown the progressive government of Jacobo Arbenz in Guatemala by backing a small force of insurgents under Colonel Castillo Armas who had crossed the border from Honduras and headed for Guatemala City. As the insurgents advanced, Arbenz's support disintegrated, and he was forced to flee into exile. Within hours, a right-wing government more to the liking of John Foster Dulles's State Department was installed. Officers of the CIA thought it would be as easy to force Castro out. They even referred to the Bay of Pigs invasion plan as "Operation Guatemala" and bragged that the only difference would be that "this time our boys will come in by sea rather than by land."

The Bay of Pigs invasion was, as one observer called it, that rarest of things: a perfect failure. The plan was poorly conceived, poorly executed and fatally based on a wholly false assumption: that the invasion would immediately spark a popular uprising. Like Narciso Lopez in 1851, the planners were deluding themselves. Castro still had the enthusiastic support of the overwhelming majority of the Cuban people at that point. There were dissidents, yes, but they were neither organized nor armed, and most had no idea an invasion was even in the works. In many cases, their first news of it came when Cuban intelligence officers appeared at their doors to place them under arrest. In the first forty-eight hours after the invaders came ashore, an estimated 100,000 Cubans were arrested. Already identified as malcontents or "counterrevolutionaries," they were rounded up and accused of conspiring with the invaders. The majority were soon released, but thousands remained in prison for years. If the Bay of Pigs had any lasting result, it was the destruction of the still fledgling anti-Castro underground. It never recovered from the blows which fell upon it on April 17 and 18 of 1961. From that point until 1989, internal opposition was never anything over which Castro had to lose sleep. For all practical purposes, none was left.

Over the years it has been argued that the invasion might have succeeded had President Kennedy agreed at the last minute to provide U.S. air cover for the invasion force. But even the most rudimentary analysis dispels that idea. Kennedy inherited the invasion plan from the Eisenhower Administration. His biographers, most of whom were members of his inner circle, concur that he did not like it. He agreed to go ahead with the plan as long as no U.S. forces were involved in a combat role. Though aware of this strict prohibition, apparently the CIA planners thought they could change the President's mind if the Cuban-exile brigade got in trouble, as it was bound to do. When that moment came, however, the President would not budge. Nor would it have appreciably changed the outcome even if Kennedy had relented and ordered U.S. carrier planes to protect the invaders. Such support might have enabled the 1,500-man brigade to consolidate a beachhead and hold it for a few days. Eventually, however, the invaders would have been overwhelmed by Castro's immensely superior army of more than 60,000 armed with Soviet tanks and heavy artillery.

In the final analysis, there was probably only one way the invasion could have succeeded: that is, if the Cuban-exile brigade had been followed ashore by a U.S. invasion force of at least 100,000 men. At the time, many observers (as well as participants) fully expected that to happen. Speculation ran that the brigade would establish a beachhead, then the Cuban Revolutionary Council in Miami, the so-called government in exile, would be flown in. It would declare itself the legitimate government of Cuba and call for U.S. support, at which point Marines would begin to disembark. U.S. casualties would have been high and the political cost around the world even higher. The United States would have been accused of a thinly disguised act of aggression and perhaps condemned by the United Nations. Still, as it was only with direct U.S. troop involvement that the invasion was likely to succeed, many observers reasoned that such must be the plan. But it was not. There were no Marine divisions waiting offshore and no airborne divisions at planeside in southern airbases. The 1,500-man Cuban brigade was the sum total of the potential invasion force.

Castro was astounded. He had expected to face the full might of the United States. He commented to an American newsman years later, "For the first day or two we kept waiting for the real invasion force to appear. Surely the Americans were not so stupid as to invade us with only these 1,500 traitors. Surely they did not take us so lightly as that. But it soon became clear that they had indeed miscalculated, that they had expected these few *gusanos* [or worms, the Cuban term for counterrevolutionaries] to defeat the Revolutionary Armed Forces. How foolish!"

The Soviets were also surprised. They too had assumed the United States would use its own armed forces rather than allow the invasion to fail. When it did not,

The Malecón.

To Americans

old enough to

remember, this

lover's walk evokes

memories of a very

different Havana.

they may have questioned U.S. resolve. If so, the Soviets soon learned that U.S. resolve remained strong, when a miscalculation on their part led to the October, 1962, missile crisis.

Even in retrospect, the degree to which Cuba dominated U.S. foreign policy and played a central role in some of the most dramatic events of our national life is simply astonishing. Even more astonishing was the way in which one event seemed to lead to another, like a badly written Greek tragedy. The failure of the Bay of Pigs invasion was President Kennedy's darkest hour, his masterful handling of the Cuban missile crisis his finest; yet without the former, the latter probably would not have taken place. Soviet doubts about U.S. resolve may have been an element in their decision to secretly place missiles in Cuba. After all, it made little sense to emplace them unless the Soviets assumed that if the United States belatedly discovered them, it could be cowed into acquiescence.

Washington's own reaction to the failure at the Bay of Pigs also played a role in the Soviet decision. Stung by its defeat, Washington initiated Operation Mongoose, a CIA-run campaign against Cuba that included efforts to assassinate Cuban leaders, exile raids against the island, sabotage efforts and stepped-up propaganda attacks. Brigadier General Edward G. Lansdale, the Mongoose chief of operations, even distributed a memorandum stating that by October, 1962, if all else failed, it might be necessary for the United States to go in with its own troops.

According to the memorandum dated February 20, 1962, and signed by Lansdale, the purpose of these actions was "to help the people of Cuba overthrow the Communist regime…and institute a government with which the United States [could] live in peace."

Lansdale's timetable called for a revolt to take place during the first two weeks in October of 1962, and he asked for an early decision concerning the direct involvement of U.S. troops in support of the revolt. Apparently, no decision was ever made in regard to that involvement, but as late as July 23, 1962, the Department of Defense assured Lansdale that it was updating its contingency plans "to insure a decisive U.S. military capability for overt military intervention in Cuba."

With this sort of thinking in the United States, the Soviet and Cuban leaders naturally interpreted Mongoose as the buildup to a new invasion. The Soviet objective in planting the missiles was to deter that invasion and to reduce the strategic advantage then enjoyed by the United States. As for the Cubans, deterrence was almost certainly the central calculation behind their agreement to permit the emplacement of the missiles on Cuban soil.

The Cuban and Soviet governments reached a general understanding on the deployment of the missiles in May, 1962, and by July had worked out a formal agreement. Construction equipment, surface-to-air missiles to protect the major missile sites and support troops began arriving in Cuba in August and September. They were duly observed by U.S. intelligence overflights. Alerted by this activity, the United States concluded that the introduction of Soviet nuclear missiles in Cuba

A reminent of Cuba's capitalist ties to the United States, the Banco Americano has been renovated for use by the Cuban government.

was imminent. Surveillance efforts increased and on October 14 a U-2 overflight brought back the first proof that Soviet medium-range ballistic missiles (MRBMs) had arrived and were being positioned at prepared sites in Cuba.

The introduction of these missiles was not only carried out in extreme secrecy, but the Soviets directly misrepresented the facts to President Kennedy. Incredibly, in a White House meeting on October 18, 1962, four days after the United States had proof of the MRBMs, Soviet Foreign Minister Andrei Gromyko assured President Kennedy that the only Soviet weapons in Cuba were purely defensive in nature.

Though angered by this effort to mislead him, President Kennedy kept a cool head. He resisted advice to bomb the sites immediately or to send in troops to destroy them. Rather, to gain time and give the Soviets a way out that would avoid a nuclear holocaust, Kennedy decided on a naval blockade. This he announced to the world in a televised speech on the evening of October 22, in which he demanded that the missiles be removed.

The world seemed poised on the brink of war. Tensions grew as Soviet ships heading for Cuba neared the U.S. blockade line. Would they defy the blockade or turn back? If they defied it, a shooting war would begin; if they turned back, the way would open to a peaceful settlement. The world breathed a sigh of relief on October 24, when the Soviet vessels halted, reversed course, then headed for home.

Shortly thereafter, the two superpower leaders worked out an understanding to end the crisis. The Soviets agreed to remove the missiles and not to reintroduce them; the United States pledged not to invade Cuba as long as the Soviets did not reintroduce offensive weaponry.

It should be noted that despite the extreme tensions of October, 1962, the Kennedy Administration handled the crisis without violating a single precept of international law or a single international agreement. Before the President actually went before the television cameras on October 22, all U.S. allies had been briefed, as had the U.S. Congress. The Soviet government itself was forewarned. A meeting of the Organization of American States was immediately convened at which the United States asked for and got the support of its hemispheric neighbors. As a result of these efforts, President Kennedy faced his Soviet adversary with the solid backing not only of his countrymen, but also of the Western world as a whole, a fact not lost on Khrushchev.

Castro was furious. Before hearing of the Kennedy-Khrushchev understanding, Castro had sent a cable to Moscow urging Khrushchev to stand firm. Castro told Khrushchev he fully expected the Americans to invade Cuba and destroy the missile sites. If that happened, he continued, then the Soviet Union should use the missiles rather than allow them to be dismantled. He fully understood the consequences for Cuba, but insisted that American aggression had to be stopped.

He implied that Cuba was prepared to sacrifice itself in order to assure a future peace.

What Castro did not know was that the Soviets could not have used the missiles even had they wished to do so. Only about half of the warheads had arrived in Cuba and none had been placed at the end of a missile. It is unlikely that Khrushchev would have used them anyway, even if the warheads had been in place. He gambled that he could face down the Americans, but he had already lost. Kennedy was not to be intimidated. Khrushchev understood full well that a nuclear war was unwinnable and wanted no part of one. Thus, he urged the Cuban leader to be patient and to realize that Kennedy's no-invasion pledge gave them what they wanted, and without a war.

Though he bitterly disagreed with Khrushchev at the time, Castro in later years acknowledged that the Soviet leader, and Kennedy, had done the right thing by reaching an accommodation and avoiding a devastating nuclear exchange.

If Castro came out of the crisis angry at the Soviets, some of the more wild-eyed Cuban exiles in the United States were furious with Kennedy, whose no-invasion pledge they saw as a betrayal. A number of CIA operatives who had worked with the exiles were also outraged, for they had become as emotionally committed to the overthrow of Castro as their exile charges. And then there was organized crime. Already antagonized by the Kennedy Administration's fierce campaign against them, certain crime bosses had a new reason to dislike the President. His no-invasion pledge blocked any hope of regaining their lost assets in Cuba. Prior to 1959, Santos Trafficante, the Mafia boss for Florida, had also controlled the action in Cuba. He was in Cuba at the time of Castro's triumph and had been jailed for several weeks by the new revolutionary government.

It is an established fact that Jack Ruby, the man who shot Lee Harvey Oswald, was a close associate of the Mafia. It is also known that Ruby visited Cuba several times as the house guest of Lewis McWillie, who managed the *Tropicana* nightclub for the Mafia, i.e., for Trafficante. There is also strong evidence that Ruby visited Trafficante during the latter's incarceration and may have been the bagman who brought the money to Cuba to buy the Mafia boss's release from prison. In any event, shortly after Ruby's second trip, Trafficante was released and returned to the United States. This is the same Santos Trafficante who was reported by one witness to have said in the Warren Commission hearings in September of 1963, "Kennedy's not going to make it to the election. He is going to be hit."

Also, after the 1975 murder of San Giancana, another Mafia chief suspected of involvement in the assassination, Trafficante is reported to have said on an FBI surveillance tape, "Now only two people are left alive who know who killed Kennedy [Trafficante was obviously one of them]. And they aren't talking."

We may never know the whole truth of the Kennedy assassination, arguably the greatest

American's 60-year domination of Cuba lasted until 1959. Today one can see the rolling relics of that American past. 1950s era Bel Airs, Fairlanes and Packards give Havana a feeling that time has somehow stopped.

The Guantanamo Naval Base

The United States Naval Base at Guantanamo Bay, on the south coast of Cuba sixty miles east of Santiago, was acquired in 1903 under the Platt Amendment as a coaling station to help protect the approaches to the planned Panama Canal. Today it is the only U.S. base maintained on the territory of a socialist country.

The base stands as something of an anomaly within an anomaly. It is the only installation of its kind in the world, locked in the time warp that is U.S. policy toward Cuba, still adversarial, still smacking of East-West confrontation. Thus, the base is very much out of sync with the pattern of international relations in the post-cold war world. In a sense, the Guantanamo Naval base is perhaps the best metaphor for the *sui generis* nature of U.S.-Cuban relations.

murder mystery in history. What is clear beyond a shadow of a doubt is that it *was* a conspiracy. Kennedy's death was not the work of a single, deranged gunman. Strong evidence points to the involvement of organized crime, right-wing Cuban exiles, and rogue elements of the CIA. Certainly the link between Trafficante and Ruby is not a coincidence.

Allegations that Castro was behind the assassination are the least credible of all. Castro had no reason to want Kennedy dead. On the contrary, he had good reason to want him alive. It is now known that in the months before the assassination, there were a number of confidential exchanges between Kennedy and Castro. Had Kennedy lived, it is entirely possible that the two would have reached some kind of *modus vivendi*. Days before he left for Dallas, Kennedy had asked the French newsman Jean Daniel to act as an emissary and tell Castro that he was prepared to explore the possibilities of an accommodation between the two countries. Castro's reaction was an enthusiastic yes. He asked Daniel to tell Kennedy he was prepared to make important concessions in order to reach such an accommodation. Then, on Daniel's last day in Cuba, word came that Kennedy had been killed. Castro was devastated and remarked morosely to Daniel that now an easing of tensions would probably not be possible.

Though there is no confirmatory evidence, Kennedy's confidential contacts with Castro may have triggered the assassination plan. If word of these contacts leaked out through the U.S. intelligence community to the exiles and the Mafia, it might indeed have been the final straw. Already livid over Kennedy's no-invasion pledge, knowledge that he was moving towards an understanding with Castro might have persuaded them to act.

Castro's prediction that accommodation was now unlikely proved correct. Kennedy had been prepared to negotiate with Castro; Lyndon Johnson was not. U.S.-Cuban relations thus settled into a deep freeze of mutual hostility for over a decade. Though only ninety miles apart, the two countries were as alienated and distant from one another as if they were at opposite poles of the earth.

As Cuban efforts to overthrow the other governments of the hemisphere seemed to be winding down, there were some secret talks under the Ford Administration in 1975 to explore the possibilities for improved relations. These broke down quickly, however, because of Cuba's intervention in the Angolan Civil War. There was no real opening in relations between the two nations until 1977, with the Carter Administration. President Jimmy Carter indicated a willingness to establish a new relationship with Cuba, provided that Cuban troops began leaving Angola and that Castro released his political prisoners. The United States and Cuba did not formally reestablish diplomatic relations; instead, they opened interests sections ❋ in one another's capitals. The U.S. mission was technically part of the Swiss embassy and the Cubans' part of the Czech embassy in Washington. The effect was to give the United States and Cuba diplomatic relations in all but name. Since 1977, each

A shrimp boat from Miami carries Cuban refugees to Florida. Castro opened the port of Mariel on April 19, 1980 to Cubans wishing to go to the United States. By the time the exodus was halted in September, 125,000 had left the island.

❋ When one country breaks diplomatic relations with another, it normally appoints a protecting power to manage its affairs in the country from which it is withdrawing. When the United States broke diplomatic relations with Cuba in 1961, for example, it turned its affairs over to the Swiss embassy. An interests section is a relatively new embellishment on this time-honored practice, under which diplomats of the country that has broken relations handle their government's affairs themselves, but do so, at least ostensibly, as part of the embassy of the protecting power.

BILL FRAKES © MIAMI HERALD

interests section has done everything an embassy would do except fly its own flag and call its chief "ambassador."

In addition to opening up a direct channel of communication, the Carter Administration's greatest accomplishment was to bring about the release of some 5,000 Cuban political prisoners by simply agreeing to admit into the United States those who did not wish to remain in Cuba after their release. Surprisingly, almost half of those released preferred to remain in Cuba. By that one agreement, the Carter Administration did more to improve the situation of human rights in Cuba than all other administrations combined, both those before and after.

Nonetheless, the Carter Administration's opening to Cuba broke down quickly, principally over the issue of Cuban actions in Africa. Because of the deteriorating military situation in Angola, Cuban strength was increased in mid-1977. By the end of the year, Cuban forces were also going to the support of the new Marxist regime in Ethiopia in its war with Somalia. United States concern was understandable. Turning Africa into a cockpit of superpower conflict was not in anyone's interest. Yet, with Cuba being the military ally of the Soviet Union, the presence of 60,000 Cuban troops pointed in that direction.

Washington was also concerned about the 1979 Sandinista victory in Nicaragua, which was interpreted as perhaps the beginning of a new Cuban campaign to promote revolution in Latin America. By early 1980, the Carter Administration's opening to Cuba was closed. Relations between Washington and Havana became as tense as under past U.S. administrations. Then came the Mariel Exodus.

Another myth about Cuba in the United States is that the Mariel Exodus was entirely unprovoked and came as a complete surprise to the Carter Administration. Actually, both sides contributed to the problem. With the objective of bringing in a windfall in dollars, the Cuban government decided in 1979 to allow 100,000 exiles to make return visits to Cuba in a single year. This proved to be a mistake. At a time when Cuban citizens were being asked to make new sacrifices, the arrival of 100,000 exiles, all talking about the life of material plenty they enjoyed in the United States, could only be disruptive. The result was a notable increase in pressures for emigration. Cubans began forcing their way into foreign embassies, just as they did in the summer of 1990, in an effort to get out of the country. They also began hijacking boats, often at gunpoint, forcing their crews to sail them to Florida. When they arrived, they were not charged with hijacking; rather, U.S. officials immediately granted them entry into the United States.

The Cuban government complained that this was unfair. In note after diplomatic protest note, the Cubans pointed out that they were cooperating with the United States in efforts to deter aerial hijackings. In these cases, the hijackers were arrested and tried. The Cubans demanded to know why the United States did not so deal with maritime hijackers.

When the United States did not bother to respond, Cuban Vice-President Carlos Rafael Rodriguez warned in February of 1980 that unless the United States took a position on maritime hijacking, Cuba would allow thousands of intending emigrants to depart by small boats. "If you want people in small boats," he was quoted as saying, "we can give you more than you bargained for."

The United States ignored the warning.

Castro repeated it in a public speech in March. Again, Carter ignored it.

Then in early April, the Cubans miscalculated. A policeman guarding the Peruvian embassy in Havana was killed when a group of asylum seekers tried to break through the gates in a bus. Angry with the Peruvians for not being more discriminating as to whom they gave asylum, Castro decided to remove the police guards from the embassy. Within forty-eight hours, there were ten thousand people inside and the Cubans had to place a barricade around the entire block to keep more from entering.

Castro extricated himself from this embarrassing predicament by turning the situation back on the United States. He had warned that he would allow a major exodus unless the United States took a position on maritime hijacking, but the United States had not even thought it necessary to reply, let alone to take a position. Hence, Castro opened the port of Mariel and let it be known that the Cuban exiles in Miami could send down small boats to pick up their relatives. Between April 19 when the port opened and September when the

exodus halted, 125,000 Cubans poured into the United States. At given moments, Mariel harbor was clogged with as many as twelve hundred boats from the United States.

Though Castro had warned publicly that he would do it, the Carter Administration appeared to be taken by surprise when the Mariel Exodus began. At first, President Carter said the United States would open its arms to the refugees; however, when the flow became massive, he switched to urging the exiles not to send boats. Neither Carter's pleas nor other U.S. efforts to close off the flow worked. Mariel was finally shut down in September on orders from Castro, who had realized too late that in embarrassing President Carter, he had helped open the way to the election of Ronald Reagan. Once again, Cuba had played a central role in shaping not only U.S. foreign policy, but also the internal American political debate. Carter did not lose to Reagan in the 1980 election simply because of his handling, or mishandling, of the Mariel incident. Double-digit inflation coupled with the sense of impotence flowing from the Iran hostage crisis played a more central role. But Mariel was certainly a contributing factor.

Thus America entered the Reagan era. The Reagan Administration made no pretense of wanting to negotiate with the Cubans or to lower tensions, at least not initially. Rather, it began by describing Cuba as a dark force and vowed to take action against it. Although its rhetoric was tough, aside from opening a new propaganda radio station aimed at Cuba and halting U.S. tourism to Cuba, which was not very extensive anyway, it did nothing. Indeed, near the end of the Reagan mandate, a number of issues were negotiated between the two countries. There seemed to be at least some hope that the incoming Bush Administration would continue the trend, perhaps eventually even working out a more normal relationship with Cuba.

One of several tent cities erected for Cubans who came to Florida during the Mariel boatlift. More than ten years later, the United States is still coping with the effects of this extraordinary migration of people.

CUBAN VETERANS OF THE WAR IN ANGOLA.

Cuba & The Third World

Latin America

As the result of pressures and charges that Cuba's ties with the Soviet Union were incompatible with the principle of the Inter-American system, Cuba was suspended from membership in the Organization of American States (OAS) in 1962. In 1964, a second OAS resolution called on all member states to break diplomatic and trade relations with Cuba. The United States lobbied hard for both these measures, but they might have passed even had it played a more passive role. So long as the other governments felt threatened by Castro's vow to overthrow them, such sanctions were, as they saw it, useful and appropriate. Only Mexico refused to go along. It never broke diplomatic or trade

~

In 1975 Cuban soldiers joined the Angolan fight against invading South Africa. They symbolize all that Cuba aspires to be — a major player on the world stage.

Both rebels in

Guatemala (above)

and the leftist

FMLN (opposite) in

El Salvador were

heavily supported

by Cuban arms and

training. More

recently, Cuba's zeal

for supporting armed

struggles in Latin

America seems to have

given way to a desire for

negotiated settlements.

relations with Cuba. All during the years, its embassy in Havana remained open. And probably because of that, Castro refrained from efforts to encourage guerrilla warfare in Mexico.

As Castro began to move away from the encouragement of revolution at the end of the 1960s, the rationale for isolating him also began to dissipate. By 1975, a number of other countries had already joined Mexico in defying the OAS ban on relations. Before the leak became a flood, the OAS put it to a vote. By an overwhelming majority, the so-called multilateral sanctions were lifted. It would now be up to each member to decide whether or not it wished to have relations. Even the U.S. voted with the majority, though it did not itself go on to reestablish either diplomatic or trade relations.

From that point forward, Cuba was no longer a pariah; rather, increasingly, it was accepted as a member of the family returning to the fold. The Colombian Ambassador in Havana, Clara Ponce de León, put it most eloquently in 1979:

> Cuba has chosen a different political system but remains a sister republic. It is entirely appropriate, and in fact in everyone's interest, including the United States, that we treat her as a member of the family again if she wishes to be so treated and provided she adheres to the basic rules of not meddling in her neighbors' affairs. What could be gained by continuing to exclude her? Nothing. To do so would be to take a false position and to deny the instincts of blood and history which bid us stretch forth our hand to a sister with whom we have quarreled but who is nonetheless one of us.

The Latin American governments were not put off by Cuba's support for the Sandinistas' struggle against the Somoza dictatorship in Nicaragua. They could hardly have been: Many of them — notably Costa Rica, Venezuela, Panama, Colombia and Mexico — also assisted the Sandinistas. They were concerned, however, that the Cubans and the Soviets might view the Sandinista triumph as proof that armed struggle worked after all and ought to be given a new trial in other countries. Cuba, they feared, might then go back to the tactics of the 1960s — perhaps this time supported more tangibly by Moscow. For a brief period after the Sandinista victory, Cuban and Soviet theoreticians *did* seem to toy with the idea that armed struggle was the only feasible path to victory. Certainly that idea popped up in a number of Soviet and Cuban journals in 1980. The idea was not embraced by the two governments, however. It did not become policy and it was dropped altogether, even by the theoreticians, after the failure of the so-called final offensive of the Salvadoran guerrillas in January of 1981.

The whole question was put to rest in 1982 at a conference of communist and revolutionary parties in Havana. There it was agreed that the conditions for armed struggle existed only in two Latin American countries, El Salvador and Guatemala. Henceforth, only in those countries would it be considered even doctrinally correct to support guerrilla movements. Guatemala was later dropped from the category after an election there in 1984, and in recent years Cuba has expressed its preference for a negotiated settlement even in El Salvador. This is a far cry, then, from Cuban policy of the 1960s.

That the other governments of the region no longer feel threatened by Cuba is seen in the fact that the majority of them now have full diplomatic and trade relations with the island. Since 1988, there has even been a strong sentiment among them to reincorporate Cuba as a member of the Organization of American States. Twenty years ago this would have been unthinkable — on both sides. The Latin American states considered Cuba a pariah. Cuba described the OAS as "the ministry of American colonies." Obviously, both parties have changed their minds.

C u b a & A f r i c a

As Cuba's hopes of winning revolutionary victories in Latin America withered, its attention turned increasingly to Africa. Cuba's interest in Africa is hardly surprising, given its ties of blood and history with the continent. The majority of the Cuban population is of African descent, the great-grandchildren of slaves brought over in centuries past. Several experts, including Carlos Moore, author of *Castro, The Blacks and Africa* and a noted authority on the subject, says that blacks constitute some 65% of the Cuban population. This contradicts the official census figures which place the percentage closer to one-third. The reason for this is quite simple. Over the years, white census takers, wishing to portray the country as having a white majority, have tended to classify mulattoes and light-skinned Afro-Cubans as white. In hopes of bettering their lot by passing as white, many Afro-

The last Cuban soldiers arriving home from the war in Angola. Raúl and Fidel Castro (opposite) have exported revolution in accordance with their own goals and principles.

Cubans have fully cooperated in the practice, often taking the initiative by indicating their color as white. Nevertheless, Cuba would not be Cuba without the influence of African music, myth, art and religion.

Since the earliest days of the Cuban Revolution this heritage has been glorified. This was politically astute on Castro's part. In addition to its sentimental bonds with Africa, Cuba had more concrete interests and objectives there. Essentially Castro wanted to win political influence and to enhance Cuba's leadership role in the Third World. Playing up Cuba's African heritage helped solidify Afro-Cuban support for Castro's Revolution. It was also useful in identifying Cuba as a Third World country and in establishing a rationale for Cuba's involvement in Africa.

That involvement began almost the moment Castro came to power. Even during the struggle against Batista, he provided small amounts of military assistance to the Algerian freedom fighters in their struggle to gain independence from France. Upon their victory, Cuba was one of the first countries to establish relations with the new government in Algiers. In 1963, Cuba sent a small contingent of troops to fight on Algeria's side in the first Algerian-Moroccan War. Then the next year, Ché Guevara visited most of the so-called progressive countries in Africa in an effort to set up an anti-imperialist alliance. Nothing came of the alliance, but it was during this swing through Africa that Guevara established the first strong ties with the Angolan Popular Liberation Movement (MPLA).

In the wake of a South African invasion of Angola in 1975, Castro began providing troop support for the MPLA, and Cuban troops eventually turned the tide of battle. Though the Ford Administration labeled Cuban involvement in Angola as "unprovoked aggression," it did not voice a word of protest when the South Africans invaded Angola. Indeed, according to John Stockwell, the chief of the CIA's Angola Task Force at the time, the Ford Administration not only had prior knowledge of the South African invasion, but also maintained close liaison with the invading force.

The MPLA became the government of the independent Angolan state, one which naturally had a close and special relationship to Cuba. While the Ford Administration was not pleased with this outcome, Castro's stock in the Third World soared. The conflict was seen by the Third World as a struggle between the MPLA and racist South Africa. Cuba could not lose politically by going to the assistance of the MPLA. Shortly after the Angolan intervention, Havana was designated as the site for the next Non-Aligned Summit Meeting, an honor which meant that Castro would become chairman of the Non-Aligned Movement.

Reaction in the Third World to Castro's intervention on the side of Ethiopia in the Somalia-Ethiopian War of 1977–78 was more mixed. While Cuban involvement in Angola was largely a Cuban endeavor, Cuba's intervention in the Horn of Africa was clearly a joint Soviet-Cuban operation. Thus, Cuba was perceived as serving the interests of one of the superpowers, rather than coming in as one Third World state helping another, as in Angola. Cuba's actions in the Horn, therefore, were seen in a less positive context.

There was no doubt, moreover, that Castro's actions displeased the Carter Administration.

The reality today is that all Cuban troops have long since left Ethiopia. And, as a result of an agreement reached in December, 1988, all troops have left Angola as well. The Cubans returned home with a sense of having accomplished what they were sent to do. Somalia has given assurance that it will not again attack Ethiopia, and the South African threat to Angola has been neutralized.

The departure of Cuban forces from Africa removed one of the most contentious issues between the United States and Cuba. Indeed, the Cubans thought that by negotiating an end to their troop presence in Africa, they were laying the groundwork for a more normal relationship with the United States, which for years put forward the removal of Cuban troops as a condition for improved relations. Once the Cubans were out of Africa, however, the Bush Administration took the position that conditions for improving relations still had not been met.

What were Cuba's interests and objectives around the globe? Essentially, to win political influence and to enhance Cuba's leadership role within the Third World. Castro's image of himself was not as the leader of a small Latin American country. Rather, he saw himself as a major international actor and Cuba as an important Third World power, one with alliances in Africa and the Middle East as well as in the socialist world. Indeed, Cuba's ability to project its military and political influence into far corners of the globe did tend to set it apart from other Third World countries. To the irritation of many — including Henry Kissinger, who once complained that Cuba was a "little" country and had no right to such a policy — Cuba often seemed to be playing a role once reserved for great powers.

MARICE COHN BAND © MIAMI HEARALD

A MEMBER OF THE WORLD CHAMPION CUBAN
VOLLEYBALL TEAM

Race, Religion & The Revolution

The struggle of black Cubans for freedom and equality within their own country has been long and bloody — and it has not yet ended. Blacks have come far since the slave revolt of 1849 and the black uprising of 1912 in Oriente province. Even before the Revolution gained power in 1959, color lines were blurred. Whites and blacks fraternized more easily in Cuba than in the United States.

~

The Revolution gave Cuba's black population equal rights and opportunities. As a result, they are among Castro's most loyal supporters.

There was little segregation in public places, though the practice continued at private clubs and beaches. Universities were open to blacks, and in theory blacks could hold any job. President Batista himself was a mulatto. However, in reality the poorest 20% of the population was mostly Afro-Cuban. There were few black professionals; rather, they were relegated to menial jobs and manual labor. Residual color lines remained, moreover. Even as president, Batista could not belong to the Havana Yacht Club: no blacks or mulattoes were allowed.

The Revolution changed a great deal. Institutionalized color lines were done away with almost immediately. No longer was anyone barred from membership in anything because of his or her race or color.

Without question, blacks have benefitted from the Revolution. Now there is much greater social and employment mobility. There are many black professionals and as many blacks in graduate school as whites. Yet, strangely, the picture remains ambiguous. While those of African descent constitute the majority of the population, they are grossly under-represented in the top levels of the Cuban government and the Communist party. At the end of the 1980s there were only two blacks on the fourteen-member Politburo and only three on the thirty-one member Council of State. Of the ninety-five generals in the Cuban Army, only four were black.

After the Revolution, Cuban officials argued that under-representation was simply the result of culture lag. The argument ran that Afro-Cubans had never had the educational advantages of whites; hence, they were not as well prepared. And it would take them years to catch up, years in which blacks would not be appropriately represented at the top. A logical argument in the sixties, it no longer holds water thirty years after the Revolution. A generation has come and gone, plenty of time to close the gap. To remedy the situation, Castro announced at the Third Party Congress in 1985 that active measures would be taken to include more Afro-Cubans in the Central Committee. "In order for the Party's leadership to duly reflect the ethnic composition of our people," the Congress document read, "it must include those patriots of proven revolutionary merit and talents who in the past have been discriminated against because of their skin color."

It does not seem possible that blacks could have been discriminated against by the Revolution itself. And yet, they obviously have been, to the point that the party felt it necessary to adopt what amounts to an affirmative-action program in 1985 to redress that ill.

Some Afro-Cubans have their own explanation. They feel Castro is genuinely interested in raising up the under-privileged classes, which certainly include blacks. And, while he has no animosity towards Afro-Cubans, his attitude remains that of his Galician father and grandfathers, essentially paternalistic. It is all well and good to give blacks access to education and better jobs, but actual empowerment is something else again.

If Fidel has been guilty of a paternalistic attitude toward Cuba's black majority, he seems to have belatedly realized it or wished to do something about it. The affirmative-action program is one such effort. A change in the government's

Though the Revolution has greatly improved the status of blacks in Cuban society, there remains a lack of representation in high level positions.

attitude toward *Santeria* as a religious expression may be considered another. In the past, the government treated *Santeria* as an interesting cultural phenomenon that attracted tourists, even though it was discouraged as a religious movement. But it has remained a powerful religious movement on the island. In 1985, a high official of the Catholic Church in Cuba estimated that as much as 85% of the population, if not actually worshiping African deities, at least had a healthy respect for them. Practicing Catholics might light a candle in the morning for *La Caridad del Cobre*, the patron saint of Cuba. Then that night, just to be sure, they might also sacrifice a pigeon to *Cachita*, her alter ego, who is really *Oshum* the mulatta goddess of pleasure.

Until recently, the government frowned on both religions, but was more tolerant of the Catholicism than the practices of *Santeria*. A sign that official attitudes were changing appeared in 1987 when the government invited Olubuse II of Nigeria to visit Cuba. Olubuse is the *Ooni*, or spiritual leader, of the *Lucumi* faith, the principal *Santeria* sect in Cuba. In the context of religion, this gesture had the same importance as a visit by the Pope would have. Received by Fidel Castro himself, Olubuse apparently was assured greater latitude for the practice of the *Lucumi* faith. In return, Olubuse praised Castro for "creating a society free from racial discrimination."

Whatever the precise terms of the understanding between Castro and Olubuse, since the *Ooni's* visit, the government has increasingly accepted the practice of *Santeria* as a religion.

Castro's new tolerance of *Santeria* may result from pragmatic political considerations. Cuba is facing increasing difficulties, a troubled economy, and the collapse of the communist world which it once counted on for support, including the disruption of its economic ties to the Soviet Union. Therefore, Castro may have calculated that now more than ever he needs the unreserved support of the Afro-Cuban majority. Opening the doors to a religion most have tenaciously clung to over the years is a clever way of appealing for that support.

As a result, the government seems to have increased the determination of the Afro-Cuban majority to defend the Revolution. Even Carlos Moore, an Afro-Cuban exile who lives in Martinique and has long been a critic of the Castro government, recently acknowledged that,

> While one may criticize Castro on many counts, the fact that the
> Afro-Cuban population has scored tremendous gains under the
> Revolution is unquestioned. The last thing Afro-Cubans want is a
> return to the old days, to the system that existed prior to the
> Revolution; rather, they want real equality. They want represen-
> tation that reflects their majority role, and they want the freedom
> to practice their traditional religions. If Castro can assure them
> that the Revolution is moving toward both goals, I have no doubt
> that Afro-Cubans would fight for the Revolution....If the con-
> servative white exiles from Miami got back in power, it would
> mean the end of all the gains Afro-Cubans have made since 1959.

Clearly, if Castro can keep the Afro-Cuban community on his side, they could be the key to assuring the survival of his faltering regime. On the other hand, should he lose that support, they could easily trigger his downfall.

Religion in Cuba

The most sacred

symbol for Cuban

Catholics is the

Church of the

Virgin which sits

atop a hill in the

village of El Cobre.

The relationship between the Cuban Revolution and other religions has long been a troubled one. Castro expelled all foreign clergy in 1961, closed down many churches and parochial schools and nationalized most other church property. Many Catholic priests, Baptist ministers and Jehovah's Witnesses soon found themselves behind bars. This clash between church and state was not based on ideology per se. In fact, it occurred before Castro had even moved to adopt the Marxist–Leninist system. As Jesuit priest Father Francisco Guzman commented at the time, "Castro insists that the Revolution is the supreme deity to which all else must be subordinated. We of course cannot accept such a view. We know that another deity is supreme."

Castro's conflict with the Catholic Church damaged his popularity with the Cuban people, very little, if at all. Though most Cubans were nominally Catholic, few took the church very seriously. Men rarely went to church at all, except to be baptized and buried — and to attend their daughter's wedding.

Many nominal Catholics preferred the practice of *Santeria*, which made none of the strait-laced moral demands of the Christian churches. Quite the contrary, among the most visible African deities were those of the sensual pleasures. There is nothing *Oshum*, or *Cachita*, likes better than a good time.

Certainly very few Cubans wanted to be Catholic priests. As of 1961, more than 450 of the some 725 priests in Cuba were Spanish — a fact that reminded Cubans of something that had undermined the position of the church even before the turn of the century: that is, the church had supported Spain during the wars of independence and therefore was not identified with the forces of Cuban nationalism.

Once Cuba adopted the Marxist–Leninst faith, which described religion as the opiate of the people and the priests and ministers as "shaman exploiters," the plight of believers became even more difficult. By definition, they were outside the system and often became objects of derision and scorn, or worse. Further, in order to get ahead in the system, one had to be a member of the Communist party, or at least indicate acceptance of its tenets. As believers could not do this, they tended to be relegated to the lower paying jobs.

The situation began to change in 1980 when Fidel Castro went to the celebration in Managua of the first anniversary of the Sandinista revolutionary triumph. There he met priests who were actually members of the revolutionary government and who convinced him that the basic teachings of Marxism and Christianity were compatible. They explained that the church, or at least powerful elements within it, were now on the side of the poor and the downtrodden. How could he doubt, they asked? Just look at the martyred priests and nuns in El Salvador. Just look at Archbishop Oscar Romero, gunned down at his altar because he had championed the humble.

Upon his return to Cuba, Castro announced that henceforth the Revolution would explore ways of working out a more congenial and mutually beneficial relationship with the churches. A dialogue began with the Catholic Church and with the various Protestant faiths, and soon an Office for Religious Affairs was set up within the Central Committee. In an interview with Brazilian priest Frei Betto, which was given wide dissemination in Cuba, Fidel Castro stressed his own religious education and praised the efforts of the Church on behalf of the

poor in other countries. The Cuban government would henceforth respect the beliefs of all, Castro said, as long as those beliefs did not harm or undermine the Revolution. If the Cuban people had been looking for a signal from Castro as to how they were supposed to react to things religious, they now had it. Co-existence and reconciliation became the watch words.

Still, problems remain. There are not nearly enough seminarians to replace Cuba's aging priests, and there are not enough priests to minister to a Cuban population which shows signs of renewed commitment to religion. Though, of course, believers are no longer officially discriminated against, one cannot legislate attitudes. Many believers complain that some of their fellow citizens continue to treat them as pariahs. Many churches remain closed or are in serious disrepair. Parochial schools remain unthinkable. The government has

not evolved that far.

While many problems remain, much progress has been made. There is far greater respect for freedom of religion in Cuba today than there was ten years ago. By the end of another decade, perhaps there will be full freedom.

Santeria flourishes in a socialist state where atheism is the official doctrine, but where Afro-Cubans are the majority. Eugenio Lamar (left), a priest of Santeria, stands with his cabinet of saints.

Cuba Today

The grave of José Martí

in Santiago de Cuba.

Alejo Alvarez (below)

is a member of the

Citizen s Militia at

the Bay of Pigs.

For Alvarez and many

older Cubans the

Revolution is still alive.

To them recent economic

sacrifices are another

chance to carry on

the good fight.

Passing the time on the streets of Trinidad, Cuba. A common sight, a bird cage (below), adorns a wall along an avenue of the city.

A dancer at the Tropicana evokes memories of the same bourgeois decadence that fanned the fires of revolution only thirty years ago.

The H. Uppman

Tobacco Factory in Old

Havana. Tobacco is a

labor intensive industry

that has changed little

in the last century.

All cigars are hand

made. The entire

process involves around

a hundred different

stages from the time

the tobacco leaves

arrive at the factory.

A ferry (below) crosses

Havana Harbor.

Valentin Perez, (left) a shoemaker at his shop El Charol in Cardenas. Children (above) on the streets of Trinidad, Cuba.

Two women (below) meet in the doorway of one of the brightly colored and ornate homes of Old Havana.

Morro Castle

(above) guards the

entrance to Havana

Harbor. It is a

reminder of four

centuries of Spanish

colonial rule. The

Havana skyline

at dusk (right).

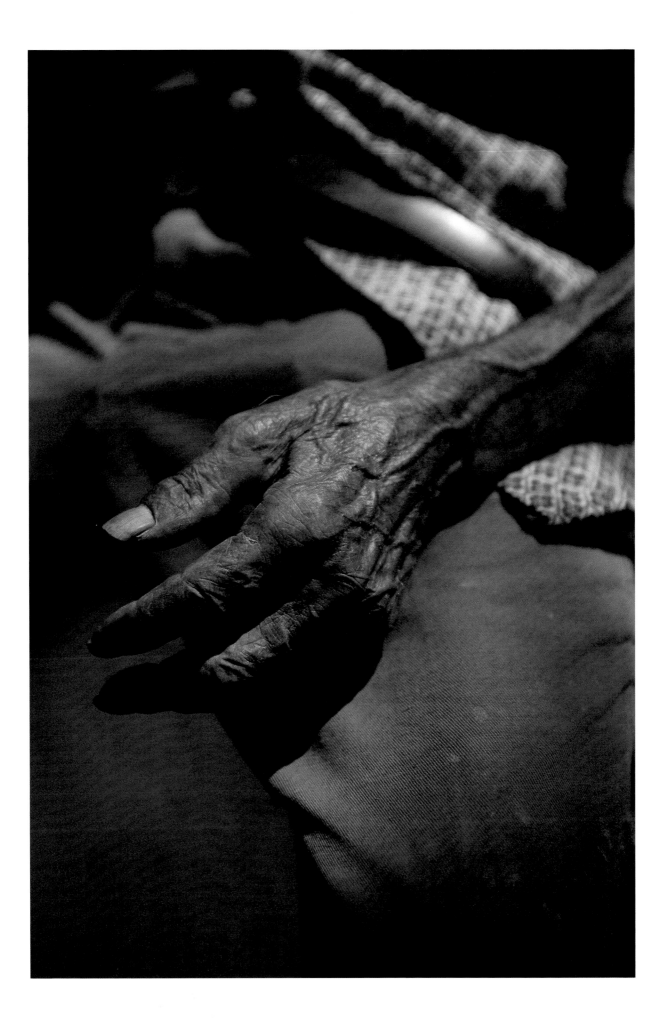

An
Economy of
Circumstance

While the Cuban economy under Fidel Castro has had problems over the years, until recently its performance on balance was quite respectable. During the period 1962–85, it registered an average annual growth rate of 5%, one of the highest in Latin America. In the mid-1980s, Cuba was hit by the same debt/interest-rate crisis as the rest of the developing countries: Prices for export commodities fell at the same time interest rates rose. As a result, Cuba's growth rate plummeted severely.

Since 1989, this adverse situation has been compounded by the disruption of its preferential trade with Eastern Europe as well as uncertainties concerning its trading relation-

~

A laborer waits for his ride to work. The collapse of communist Eastern Europe and uncertainties in the Soviet Union have compromised Cuba's economic future.

For two centuries

sugar cane has been the

mainstay of the Cuban

economy. For all that

time, it has been both

a blessing and a curse.

Pack horses (below)

deliver food to remote

villages in the Sierra

Maestra mountains.

FRED WARD © BLACK STAR

ship with the Soviet Union. The Soviet Union is not likely to eliminate that trade, from which it benefits also. But the Soviet economy and transportation system are in such disarray that shortfalls are inevitable. Soviet planners cannot get bread to Moscow, much less assure deliveries of petroleum, wheat and other commodities to a far-away island.

Sugar remains the mainstay of the economy, as it has been for almost two centuries. During the decade before Castro came to power, 1948–58, sugar represented an average 84.1% of total Cuban exports. Continued reliance on sugar was not part of Castro's plan: rather, he at first announced that Cuba would industrialize and diversify its agriculture sector.

Industrialization, however, has proven far more difficult than Castro had imagined. Cuba has few raw materials to speak of, no sources of energy, and only a small internal market. Diversification of agricultural products was technically feasible but was not pushed after the first few years of the Revolution because the Soviet Union encouraged Cuba to produce more sugar, not less. As a consequence, Cuba made no effort to become self-sufficient in foodstuffs. Following that bit of Soviet direction has cost Cuba dearly. With its trade links to the Soviet Union now disrupted, and without hard currency to buy food elsewhere, Cuba is simply no longer able to feed its people adequately. Producing more food is critical if the Revolution is to survive.

Meanwhile, the whole future of sugar as an export commodity is dismal. Sweeteners can be made more cheaply from corn than from sugar, and countries that once imported sugar have become net exporters. Unfortunately, Cuban economic planners have moved sluggishly to address this problem. Sugar still accounts for 75% of Cuba's exports.

Government officials are now trying to change that. Taking advantage of Cuba's highly literate labor force, planners are endeavoring to increase the role of nontraditional exports and to develop a major biotechnology sector, with the idea of becoming the principal supplier of medicines to the Third World. Brazil is already a big buyer of Cuban medicines, as are a number of African states.

In the quest for new sources of revenue, Cuban planners are also counting heavily on expansion of the tourist industry, which has long been a major hard-currency earner. But if Cuba is to attract large numbers of tourists, resort facilities must be expanded and Havana will need extensive renovation. When Castro came to power in 1959, he considered Havana a parasite on the flank of the nation and diverted resources to the countryside for schools, clinics and roads. Thirty years of neglect is apparent everywhere in the city. Buildings are unpainted, mortar crumbles from walls, and elevators and other equipment rarely work. The Cuban government has embarked on an ambitious face-lift, but it comes at a time when resources for construction are increasingly scarce.

Service and facilities aside, the "infrastructure" of Cuba's tourist industry is its natural setting. The white sand beaches are among the most beautiful in the world. The diving is spectacular, but perhaps nowhere more so than just off *Punta Frances* on the Isle of Youth, where huge grouper and colorful tropical fish live in groves of black coral. Further down the coast, wrecks of Spanish galleons sit underwater with their cannon still precisely spaced, just as they were before the decks rotted.

Besides rich soil, Cuba is blessed with sunshine year round and the most beautiful beaches in the world. Cuba wants the world to rediscover the island's charms to bring in tourist dollars badly needed for economic salvation.

After thirty years of neglect, Havana finds itself in need of renovation at a time when resources are scarce.

Ashore, there is the haunting beauty of the Viñales Valley in Pinar del Rio province, with its hills jutting up dramatically from the eroded valley floor. The green soaring mountains of the Oriente province plunge directly into the turquoise sea. And from one end of the island to the other, there are the rolling hills and tall rustling palms that so enchanted Christopher Columbus almost five hundred years ago.

Even though rundown, Havana still has its attractions. The *Tropicana* nightclub and restaurants such as the *La Bodeguita del Medio* and *El Floridita* remain popular. Faded pictures of Ernest Hemingway, Errol Flynn and other American celebrities who frequented these places still hang on the walls and bring back memories of a

far different Cuba. Errol Flynn spent almost every night during late 1958 and early 1959 at a corner table of the *Bodeguita*. Subsequently, he was to claim that he had been in the mountains with Fidel. If so, other patrons will attest, it was a quick trip, for there were few evenings when the Flynn table was not occupied.

What is now required is not that tourism become an important source of hard currency, but that it come to rival sugar as the principal source. Still, without access to its largest and most natural market, the United States, it is difficult to see how the Cuban tourist industry can reach anything like its real potential. As long as American tourists are forbidden by their government from travelling to Cuba, the Cuban tourist industry will, in a sense, be operating at half-speed.

One thing the Cubans do to expand and improve their tourist facilities is to invite foreign private investors to participate in joint ventures with the Cuban government. Some fifty-five of these enterprises are already in operation and many others are in the process of negotiation, with capital provided by entrepreneurs from Spain, Canada, France, Japan, Mexico and Jamaica. Though the experiment began in the tourist industry, joint ventures are planned in other sectors of the economy as well. In time, these ventures may change the face of the Cuban economy.

Certainly economic prospects would be improved if reports of oil reserves off the Cuban coast prove accurate. In the midst of its most serious economic challenge since the

Nearly every ship in Havana Harbor is Soviet. Since the early sixties, these ships have provided the trade, services and arms that have kept Cuba afloat. The survival of Cuba's system in the days ahead will not depend upon the generosity of a foreign power, but on the resolve and patience of the Cuban people themselves.

1960s, and now with no powerful patron to whom it can turn, Cuba needs something like the discovery of new oil fields to reverse its economic decline. That in itself, however, might not be enough. The resuscitative impact of joint ventures, of an expanding tourist industry, of nontraditional exports and even of possible new oil production is two or three years away. Meanwhile, the Cuban government must solve the problem of food supply. If it cannot, the rest may be academic.

A LEADER OF THE CITIZENS MILITIA

Cuba in a Changing World

Doubtless 1989, 1990, and 1991 will be remembered in history as three of the most tumultuous years of the twentieth century. The Berlin Wall came down. The communist regimes of Eastern Europe collapsed and were replaced by popularly elected governments. Germany was reunited. Astonishingly, in August of 1991, in the wake of an abortive conservative coup, communist rule was abolished in the Soviet Union itself.

~

Reinforced by repeated weekend exercises and the memory of the Bay of Pigs, many Cubans still fear an invasion by the United States.

While the rest of the world cheered, Cuba could only see this train of events as ominous. The family of communist nations of which it had so long been a part was crumbling around it. And as one by one the members of the the family left the former communist homestead, they decided they no longer wished to trade with Cuba, or that they wished to do so only if Cuba could pay hard currency up front. The resulting reduction in trade with Eastern Europe was a blow to Cuba, but only a minor one. Of its trade with the countries of the Communist Common Market (CEMA), only 18% had been with Eastern Europe, while 82% was with the Soviet Union, including the one absolutely vital commodity, petroleum. The link with Eastern Europe was dispensable; that with the USSR was not, and as of August 1991, that too was in some jeopardy.

Added to the disappearance of communist regimes in Eastern Europe, were the ouster of Manuel Noriega — as a result of the U.S. invasion of Panama in December of 1989 — and Daniel Ortega's electoral loss in Nicaragua in February of 1990. The conviction arose among some Cuban-Americans in Miami that Castro had to be next. Immediately after the elections in Nicaragua, bumper stickers appeared in Miami with the triumphant slogan, "Yesterday Manuel, Today Daniel, Tomorrow Fidel!"

Wishful thinking among the Cuban exiles had Castro on the verge of collapse. That did not make it so. Castro had no intention of holding democratic, internationally supervised elections in Cuba as Daniel Ortega had done in Nicaragua. Also, the United States had no intention of invading Cuba as it had Panama.

Nor can the Cuban case be compared to those in Eastern Europe. Unlike the Eastern bloc leaders, Fidel Castro still has the aura of a nationalist leader and retains a good deal of popular support. There is, to be sure, disgruntlement, and if economic conditions do not improve, dissatisfaction could in time balloon into outright dissent. For the time being, however, Castro need not fear a popular uprising reminiscent of the one in Romania.

Nor does he need to fear a military coup. The arrest and execution of General Arnaldo Ochoa and three other officers and the imprisonment of a number of others in the summer of 1989 created a minor sensation at the time. Ochoa was charged with malfeasance and improper conduct, most of the others with involve-

Though Gorbachev instigated a revolution of liberalization in most of the communist world, Castro has shown little desire to embrace the ideals of glasnost and perestroika.

ment in drug smuggling. Inevitably there were suspicions that Castro himself had authorized the smuggling operation. Then, it is speculated, Castro put the blame on his subordinates and threw them to the dogs when it seemed U.S. intelligence was about to reveal hard evidence of Cuban involvement. It was believed Ochoa had simply disagreed one too many times with the Castro brothers and had come to be seen as a potential focal point of dissent — which would indeed have been worrisome, given his popularity in the Army.

Perhaps the truth will never be known. Those who may have known died in front of a firing squad. That aside, Castro does not have to worry at this point about his armed forces turning on him. The Ochoa episode may have left a bad taste in the mouths of some army officers, but there were no signs of real disaffection within the military. The armed forces seemed to remain overwhelmingly loyal to Castro. Whether they would remain so should popular discontent increase is the crucial question.

As for the Soviet Union, even in the wake of the cataclysmic events of August 1991, it is unlikely to sever its ties with Cuba completely. It has a strong interest in retaining access to its huge intelligence facility at Lourdes, and it needs the sugar and nickel it gets from Cuba. Obviously, however, it will be more difficult for Cuba to deal with a series of republics than one central Soviet government, but as the

These men have gathered to play dominos every weekend since before the Revolution. Will the generation born after 1959 continue to share the revolutionary zeal of their elders?

Cuban stevedores unload cargo from a Soviet ship. The Cuban waterfront is becoming more quiet all the time. Cuba needs to find new trading partners to replace those no longer coming from Eastern Europe.

union republics break away, that is precisely what it may have to do. Further, as of early 1991, the Soviet Union placed trade with Cuba on a hard-currency basis. That is, goods exchanged between the two countries are now valued in dollars at close to world market prices. This was designed not only to reduce any net cost to the Soviet Union, but doubtless also to neutralize domestic critics who want to end "aid" to Cuba. As of early 1991, it could be argued that aid had become trade.

Placing trade on a hard-currency basis is to Cuba's disadvantage, though not intolerably so. So long as the Soviet Union buys Cuba's sugar, nickel and citrus products for dollars, Cuba will also be in a position to import Soviet petroleum, though in painfully reduced quantities. The Soviet Union, or individual republics, are likely to continue to purchase those Cuban products for the time being, but over time bilateral trade will almost certainly decline. Meanwhile, the Soviet economy and transportation system are in such disarray that there are bound to be shortfalls in Soviet deliveries, no matter what is promised on paper.

Clearly then, even though the Soviet Union may not abandon Cuba, its economic links to the island will at best become increasingly tenuous. At worst, these economic links could be swept away by the very momentum of reaction to the failed conservative coup in August. In prudence, Cuba must plan for a future without the Soviet Union.

While for the moment the Soviets have strategic interests in Cuba, such as the Lourdes intelligence facility, they acknowledge that the island is of less and less value to a Soviet Union which is retracting within its own borders and trying to reshape its own future. Despite the present problems, however, Soviet diplomats point out that theirs is a country which still considers itself to be a great power. Thus, without some prior assurances from the United States, that it will not take advantage of the situation, Soviet officials have been reluctant to reduce military assistance to Cuba.

As Ambassador Valery Nikolayenko, then the director of the Latin American Countries Department of the Soviet Foreign Ministry, put it at a conference in Washington in late 1990:

If, in keeping with the present spirit in the world of settling disagreements through dialogue, the United States were willing to reduce tensions with Cuba and begin a diplomatic process aimed at resolving conflicts of interest and normalizing relations, then the Soviet Union could look much more seriously at the possibility of beginning to reduce — and reduce dramatically — its military assistance and the other elements of its presence on the island.

Why should the United States not begin to engage Cuba in a negotiating process? The fact that Cuba is now in difficult straits improves the United States's bargaining position. Hence, there is greater reason for the U.S. to negotiate with them.

The United States Moves the Goal Posts

Though the Reagan Administration successfully negotiated a number of issues with Cuba near the end of its term, the Bush Administration quickly ruled out diplomacy and said there would be no thaw in relations. In a speech before a Miami audience on August 16 of 1989, President Bush emphasized that the United States could not think of improving relations with Cuba until it saw some sign of change in Cuba's domestic and international policies. He lamented that so far he had seen none, claiming there was no increased respect for human rights and Cuban support for subversion in neighboring countries was as serious a problem as ever.

Such rhetoric notwithstanding, Cuba's record on human rights had improved, as was acknowledged by the Department of State in its 1989 report on human rights practices around the world. By the latter part of 1988, the gradual improvement which had begun in the mid-1970s had led to the release of almost all political prisoners. International human rights organizations estimated that no more than three hundred remained. Conditions of incarceration, moreover, had improved

Rhetoric of the Revolution. This billboard in Havana reads, "Señores Imperialistas, we have absolutely no fear of you."

markedly. So much so that the Cuban government was allowing various international delegations to tour its prisons. In September, 1988, Castro actually permitted the visit of a United Nations inspection team, which not only went through the prisons and talked to political prisoners, but also interviewed various other Cuban citizens who had complaints against the government. Castro was even grudgingly permitting a number of Cuban human rights groups to operate on the island itself.

The Cuban government's more lenient attitude was doubtless a response to international public opinion, but it also thought that progress on the human rights issue would help lay the groundwork for improved relations with the United States. Thus, when the Bush Administration rejected the possibility of any such improvement, it removed one of the Cuban government's incentives to continue movement in the right direction. A crackdown quickly followed. By late-1989, most of the Cuban human rights activists were in jail, the Cuban government had suspended the prison visits of international human rights organizations, and, finally, indicated that it would no longer cooperate with the United Nations human rights committee.

The Bush Administration's rejection of a thaw in relations was not the immediate cause of this crackdown. Rather, in an increasingly defensive mood because of the collapse of the communist world around him, Castro instinctively began to "circle the wagons." Whatever might be happening in the Soviet Union, he probably wished to signal the Cuban people — *glasnost* would not be tolerated in Cuba. As his fears have grown, he has lashed out in an almost irrational way at anything resembling a dissident voice.

On the other hand, Cuba wanted and needed better relations with the United States. Had improvement in those relations been held out as an option, it might have outweighed Castro's defensive instincts and kept the door open to continued improvement in the human rights field. By rejecting the possibility of a thaw in relations, Washington made sure that door was closed.

Human rights leaders in Cuba were aghast. Elizardo Sanchez, for example, is the chairman of the Cuban Commission on Human Rights and National Reconciliation. He has fought for the cause of human rights for years and has been in and out of Cuban prisons because of it. In 1989 he was caught up in the crackdown and again imprisoned. But even from his prison cell, he continued to advocate an easing of tensions between the United States and Cuba as a prerequisite for any liberalization process in Cuba. The linkage between the two is obvious enough. Cuba's location only ninety miles off the shores of the most powerful country in the world — a hostile superpower with which it has been locked in a bitter adversarial relationship for thirty years — makes its assessments of U.S. intentions absolutely central to all its calculations and decisions. The more Cuba feels threatened by the United States, the less likely it is to adopt moderate policies. On the contrary, Castro always reacts to U.S. pressure by demanding internal discipline and unity.

As Yndamiro Restano, one of Elizardo Sanchez's lieutenants in the human rights movement, pointed out to a visiting American in 1990, the only ones hurt by the Bush Administration's hard line were the Cuban people themselves, and especially the human rights activists. "Unless there is some change of course in Washington,"

he concluded, "we are all fried. We seem to be trapped between the hardliners on both sides."

Gustavo and Sebastian Arcos, leaders of Cuba's other major human rights organization, the Human Rights Committee, agree with Restano. Indeed, in a letter dated September 15, 1990, to exiles in Miami, Sebastian emphasized that the Cuban people want to see changes, yes, but peaceful changes brought about as the result of a great national dialogue. "Here," he said, "the people, and above all the young people, want changes, but changes from within. They fear the Americans and the

Three common modes

of transportantion

on the streets of

Varadero, Cuba.

A meat lorry delivers its precious merchandise to a butcher in Bayamo.

Cubans in Miami." He continued:

> The intelligent thing for the government of the United States to do would be to guarantee that there would never be an invasion of or any military aggression against Cuba, and to commit itself to return the Guantanamo Naval Base to the first democratic government constituted within the country. And the Cubans in Miami should not speak of vengeance, nor of settling accounts, but rather they should offer all they have and all they know to national reconstruction in all fields and senses. They should so speak that the people here would see them as a hope for a better and more secure future, and not as a threat to the little they have.

Moving and sensible words. Unfortunately, neither the U.S. government nor the conservative exiles in Miami paid them the slightest heed. Quite the opposite. When Gustavo Arcos had earlier called for a dialogue with the Cuban government, he was savagely condemned by the Cuban-American National Foundation as a "traitor."

Improving human rights was not the only way in which Cuba had addressed U.S. concerns. It had already pulled all troops out of Ethiopia and signed tripartite agreements with South Africa and Angola. Under this agreement Cuba's forces are being withdrawn from Angola as well. In addition, Castro's policies regarding revolution in Latin America have changed drastically from the 1960s. Castro long ago gave up on turning the Andes into the Sierra Maestra of Latin America. Rather than trying to overthrow the other governments of the hemisphere, Castro had reestablished diplomatic and trade relations with most of them. Only in El Salvador does Cuba maintain that supporting guerrillas is the right thing to do. And even there, Cuba has emphasized that it prefers a negotiated solution.

During the Angolan-Namibian negotiations in 1988, the Cuban delegation approached the U.S. delegation and stated its interest in negotiations which would include Central America and the question of outside arms being supplied there. The U.S. delegation reported the overture to Washington, but Washington replied that it was not interested, that no response should be made to the Cubans, and that the U.S. delegation was not to allow the issue to come up again. In other words, the Cuban offer was rejected with silence.

Despite the encouraging developments in Africa and Latin America and Cuban efforts to negotiate, the United States simply ignored these developments. In President Bush's words, Washington could see "no changes at all in Cuban policies."

To suggest that it is the U.S government rather than Cuba that has refused to negotiate is not to absolve Cuba of wrongdoing or to suggest that the disagreement between the two countries was simply part of a U.S. plot. Quite the contrary, the conflicts of interest are real and need to be addressed. The presence of Cuban troops in Africa was a concrete political problem and a matter of legitimate concern to the United States. The fact that most Cuban human rights activists are in jail is also something the United States cannot ignore. It is a wrong which must be righted before there can be any substantial improvement in relations between the two nations.

The Bush Administration has indicated, however, that it will not respond

The barbers at this shop in Santiago de Cuba collectively have 103 years experience between them.

The Café Cubano in Miami suggests the strong influence of Cuban immigrants on South Florida.

positively to any Cuban concessions short of outright capitulation. In other words, the United States will do nothing more than move the goal posts: If Cuba meets one condition, the U.S. will simply put forward another. One may wonder why the Bush Administration, unlike its predecessor, has not been willing to enter into talks with Cuba. Part of the answer no doubt lies in the fact that Cuba is one of the most emotional issues on the U.S. foreign policy agenda. The U.S. can contemplate the reestablishment of diplomatic relations with Vietnam, a country with which the U.S. fought one of the bitterest and most divisive wars in its history, but not with Cuba. It is too close. The sense of having been defied too great.

Another part of the answer, however, may have been given by a member of the Bush Administration when in an unusually candid moment he observed that there was nothing to be gained through dialogue with Cuba that would outweigh the domestic political problems the dialogue itself would create. "It would cause a firestorm among powerful elements within the Cuban-American community," he predicted.

> Why should we risk that? What could we gain? Withdrawal of Soviet military forces? Who cares? There was a time when we had to take the Soviet military presence in Cuba seriously. With the end of the Cold War, we no longer do. Certainly it would not make political sense to anger the President's Cuban-American constituents just to get a Soviet regiment or two, or even a wing of MIG's, out of Cuba. No, the best thing for us to do is simply wait a few months, or even a few years. Castro will fall sooner or later, and meanwhile we won't have to antagonize those prominent Cuban-Americans in the Republican party who are so strongly opposed to anything that smells of a dialogue with the Castro regime.

The record of its actions, plus a variety of other statements on the part of government officials, suggest that the above is a fairly accurate description of the Bush Administration's calculations. Interestingly, they reflect a new element that is different from those in the calculations of the Reagan Administration. The latter, to be sure, considered Cuba to be the darkest of the forces of darkness, the most evil member of the evil empire. The Reagan Administration also valued the support of the conservative Cuban exiles and initially avoided negotiations with Cuba. Yet, near the end of its term, when it saw that negotiations might bring about the withdrawal of Cuban troops from Angola and score other gains, the Reagan Administration risked the ire of those exiles and entered into talks.

Why has the Bush administration not been willing to do so? Ironically, because the Cold War is over. In other words, the United States once viewed Cuba as a dangerous extension of Soviet military might in this hemisphere and as its surrogate in places such as Africa. Now Cuba is seen as simply the irritating remnant of what was once a threat but is no more. Risking domestic political fallout to deal with a threat is one thing; risking it to deal with an irritant is another.

Thus for the Bush Administration, there is one overriding consideration: how a dialogue with Cuba would play domestically, especially how it would play with the Cuban-American community.

The Cuban-American Community

The one million Cubans who came to the United States after 1959 brought with them all the charm, the vitality and love of life characteristic of the people of their island homeland. Theirs has been very much a success story. Many came with nothing but the clothes on their backs. Typically, they spent the first year sweeping up the bank, the second and third as tellers, the fourth and fifth as credit managers. By the sixth year they were vice-presidents. In some cases, they ended up owning the bank.

Certainly they reshaped Miami. A sleepy town dependent on the tourist trade before 1959, it soon became the gateway to Latin America. Large American companies moved their regional offices from Caracas, Rio and Mexico City to Miami. New blood and investments, new enterprises and new ways of doing things poured into Dade County. The older residents might have preferred things as they were, but Miami was forever changed. Largely because of the influx of Cubans, it has become one of the most vibrant and cosmopolitan cities in the United States.

The Cubans almost literally brought their beloved Havana with them. One finds in Miami the same restaurants and department stores, movie houses with the same names, and TV and radio stations reminiscent of those in Havana before 1959.

Rarely are exiles known for their objectivity or moderation of thought with respect to the Marxist regime back home. The Cubans brought zest and warmth to Miami, but they also brought their hatred of the Castro regime. Surprisingly, however, a poll taken in 1988 indicated that, despite overwhelming negative reaction to the Castro regime itself,

Cuban Americans protest continued Soviet support of Castro. Rarely are exiles known for their objectivity or moderation of thought with respect to the Marxist regime back home.

C.M. GUERRERO © MIAMI HERALD

almost as many Cuban-Americans were prepared to see negotiations with the Cuban government as were opposed. There is a realization that an easing of tensions between the United States and Cuba might open the way to a liberalization process in the latter, thus leading to a better way of life for their loved ones still there.

If the Cuban-American community was split on the issue of negotiations and dialogue in 1988, it is more deeply so today. Essentially the community is divided into four broad groups. The first is made up of the most ultra-conservative elements, centering around the wealthy Cuban-American National Foundation. This group wants no dialogue of any kind with the Castro regime on the part of the Cuban-American community, the internal dissidents, and most certainly on the part of the U.S. government. This rejection of dialogue flows from the belief that what is needed is not reform but the total ouster of the existing system and everyone connected with it, and their replacement by a new leadership from the outside. He denies it, but there is a good deal of evidence to suggest that Jorge Mas Canosa, chairman of the foundation, wants to become the next president of Cuba.

It is this first group, the wealthiest and most politically powerful, that seems to have the ear of the Bush Administration. Jeb Bush, the President's son, lives in Miami and is a close associate of Mas Canosa and other top leaders of the foundation.

TV Martí was the Cuban-American National Foundation's brain child. Opponents warned that it would not work. The Cuban government would simply jam its transmissions, and besides it would violate the 1982 International Telecommunications Convention, of which the United States is a signatory. They were right. The night it went on the air in March of 1990 it was seen for all of seven minutes. Then the Cuban government began jamming. TV Martí has not been seen nor heard since. The International Telecommunications Union (ITU) advised the United States that it was indeed a violation of the 1982 convention. However, President Bush certified to the U.S. Congress that TV Martí was both effective and legal. The U.S. taxpayer to this day continues to spend $16 million annually to transmit these television programs into a black hole.

There is a second group in the Cuban-American community centered around organizations such as the Cuban Liberal Union and the Cuban Christian Democratic Party. These expatriates advocate dialogue in hopes of encouraging change without bloodshed in Cuba. Their principal objective is to convince Castro that he should hold elections. They believe that from elections all else will flow.

The third group is made up of organizations such as the Social Democratic Cuban Party and the Coordinating Organization for Human Rights. Most members in the third group have always been moderates. They advocate sweeping change in Cuba, but are prepared to see it come about slowly. Meanwhile, their principal concern is to gain greater respect for human rights. They advocate the normalization of relations between the United States and Cuba.

Finally, there are a number of organizations and individuals with no particular political agenda. They take no specific position on internal changes in Cuba, though they do advocate such philosophies as greater respect for human rights and freedom of expression. This group is comprised of such organizations as the Cuban-American Research and Study Fund. Their principal objectives are to improve conditions of travel for Cubans on both sides of the Straits of Florida, to improve television links, to open direct mail service and to promote the general easing of tensions between the United States and Cuba.

The second generation of Cuban-Americans, those born after their parents fled Cuba, tend to be much less interested in the whole issue than their parents. Few belong to any of the organizations or groups mentioned above. Fewer have any idea of what Cuba or life in Cuba is like. Fewer still have any thought of ever living there, even in a post-Castro situation. Most are curious to know more about their parents' homeland, but it is unlikely that this generation will carry on the tradition of intense political advocacy. Certainly there are few Cuban-Americans below the age of thirty who would advocate bombings or murder simply to sabotage dialogue with the Cuban government.

Unfortunately, that has not been the case with their parents' generation. With the highest number of political bombings and murders in the country, Miami was designated the terrorist capital of the United States by the Justice Department some years back. This is not surprising. Throughout the sixties, the CIA ran a huge operation out of Miami. It trained thousands of Cuban exiles as assassins, commandos and saboteurs, backing them in *la causa* (the cause, i.e. the overthrow of Castro). The CIA itself long ago gave up the cause, but its former foot soldiers have not. Rather than targeting Fidel Castro, however, they now target community members who disagree with them.

Fortunately, this seems to be a generational phenomenon. The mad bombers are dying off, and they are not being replaced by younger versions.

In retrospect, the Cuban-American community is by no means monolithic. American politicians are wrong to believe that it is. There are many who advocate some kind of dialogue with Cuba. As well there are those who virulently oppose dialogue, among them the wealthiest and most influential members of the community. However, because the numbers of those who take a more moderate position are growing and the violence so common in the past seems increasingly out of place, there is hope for the future.

~

An Uncertain Future

The Castro regime may not be on the verge of collapse, but it must seem to Fidel that the world has turned upside down. The communist family of nations has collapsed around him. Even the future of the Soviet Union itself is uncertain, especially in the aftermath of the events of August 1991. Communist rule is finished and the Soviet Union could disintegrate as a country at any time.

~

The last of a dying breed, Fidel Castro contemplates Cuba's future. More than ever, he must rely on his enigmatic qualities to keep the Revolution alive.

Certainly it can no longer assure deliveries of vital commodities to Cuba. Thus, Cuba must in prudence begin to adjust to a future without Moscow's warm security blanket.

Can Cuba survive alone? Not without sweeping changes. It must quickly become a fully competing member of the international trading community. In order to do that, it must move toward a mixed economy. A more open political system is also in order if Cuba is to be an effective participant in the world around it.

Castro is the quintessential authoritarian leader. Adjusting to a more open system will not be easy for him. On the other hand, he has shown himself in the past to be innovative and pragmatic, capable of making unpalatable changes if they were necessary for survival. Which direction will he take? Toward change, or toward a rigid adherence to the status quo? Only time will tell. In the final analysis, to leave behind a lasting legacy, Castro must begin now to modify that which he has already constructed but which is no longer functional in a changed world.

If he can adapt, then the Cuban Revolution — in a transformed state — may survive. And Castro may be remembered by history as the leader who first won Cuba's full independence from the United States, then when the moment demanded it, allowed the Cuban people to take their destinies into their own hands.

If he cannot change, if he tries to hold to a centralized economy and a rigid authoritarian political system, then the future of the Cuban Revolution will be bleak indeed. As such a Cuba became increasingly isolated and out of sync with the world around it, its economic situation would only worsen. Food riots, demonstrations, even a civil war with appalling bloodshed, loom as ominous future possibilities. Better for all concerned, the United States included, would be a peaceful transformation of Cuba from the Marxist-Leninist state it is now to a social democracy it can, in time, almost certainly become.

Whatever the outcome, whatever the shape of Cuba's future, one thing is clear: Castro's Revolution has changed the island forever. Cuba will never again be as it was before 1959. Nor will the United States be the same. The Bay of Pigs, the 1962 missile crisis, the assassination of President Kennedy, and the Mariel boatlift are all now part of our history. The face of Miami has been unalterably changed.

Occasionally as allies, more often as adversaries, Cuba and the United States have continued to react to one another, as they have done through history. Geography will always bind them. Is it possible that their interaction might ever be a constructive,

Cuban refugees seeking asylum in the United States enjoy their first sustenance after nine days adrift, May 1991.

harmonious one? Or will history carry the two toward a bloody denouement?

This is a moment of high drama in the history of Cuba. The issues are drawn; the stage is set. Wither Cuba in this vastly changed world? That is the question, and the answer will come largely from the Cuban people. In a very real sense, Cuba's fate, for the first time in its history, will be decided not in a foreign capital — not in Madrid, nor Washington, nor Moscow — but on the island itself.

At this pivotal moment,

Cubans confront an

uncertain future.

Photography Credits

© AP/Worldwide Photos
page **18**

© Blackstar/Fred Ward
pages **122**, **170** (top)

© Publimerc S.A.
pages **40-41, 43, 55-57, 62-63, 67, 70-73, 75, 79-81, 84-90, 94-107, 108** (top)
129, 136, back endsheet

© Culver Pictures Inc.
pages **36-37, 46, 48-49, 59, 64-65**

© *Our Islands and Their People*
pages **38, front endsheet**

Francis Miller, Life Magazine © 1958 Time Warner Inc.
pages **74, 78**

Robert Kelley, Life Magazine © 1958 Time Warner Inc.
page **76**

Courtesy Marita Lorenz
page **108** (bottom)

© Magnum/Glinn
pages **68-69, 82-83**

© Magnum/Henriques
page **93**

© Miami Herald
page **139**

© Miami Herald/Marice Cohn Band
pages **144-45**

© Miami Herald/Al Diaz
pages **187, 190**

© Miami Herald/Bill Frakes
page **137**

© Miami Herald/C.M. Guerrero
page **185**

© Miami Herald/Rick McCawley
page **184**

Courtesy National Archives,
pages **52-53, 58** (top)

© Sagamore Hill NHS/National Park Service
pages **51, 54**

© UPI/The Bettman Archives
pages **42, 44-45, 47, 50, 61-61, 130, 176**

Great care has been

taken to properly credit

all photo sources. Any

errors are unintentional.

Acknowledgments

The author wishes to express appreciation to a number of area specialists from whose writings the resent work drew heavily. They are: Carlos Moore, author of *Castro, the Blacks and Africa*; Louis Perez, *Cuba Between Empires: 1878–1902*; Sir Hugh Thomas, *Cuba: The Pursuit of Freedom*; Tad Szulc, *Fidel: A Critical Portrait*; and Andy Zimbalist, *Cuba's Socialist Economy Toward the 1980s*.

Turner Publishing, Inc. would like to thank the following people who helped to make this book possible:

Carlos A. Gonzalez Carrasco, Francisco Usallam, Alfredo Pereira Ramirez, Osvaldo Salas, Mr. Baxter, Gilberto Caballero, Danylo Sirio, Antonio Valdes Cantara, Elizabeth Noriega, Jenie Barraclough, George Carey, John Savage, Ira Miskin, Kurt Wofingner, and all the people of Cuba whose spirit and lust for life made this book a remarkable experience.

~ Michael Reagan

Turner Publishing, Inc. would also like to thank the following people: Katherine Bird, Laura Heald, Lisa E. Oliver, Jerry Litofsky, Ken Mowry, Frédéric DeWulf, Ann Cabay-Walsh.